Pride and Prejudice

JANE AUSTEN

Level 5

Retold by Evelyn Attwood
Series Editors: Andy Hopkins and Jocelyn Potter

Pearson Education Limited
Edinburgh Gate, Harlow,
Essex CM20 2JE, England
and Associated Companies throughout the world.

ISBN 0 582 41935 2

First published in the Longman Simplified English Series 1945
First published in Longman Fiction 1993
This adaptation first published 1996
This edition first published 1999

Third impression 2001

NEW EDITION

This edition copyright © Penguin Books Ltd 1999
Cover design by Bender Richardson White

Set in 11/14pt Bembo
Printed in Spain by Mateu Cromo, S.A. Pinto (Madrid)

Published by Pearson Education Limited in association with
Penguin Books Ltd, both companies being subsidiaries of Pearson Plc

For a complete list of the titles available in the Penguin Readers series please write to your local
Pearson Education office or to: Marketing Department, Penguin Longman Publishing,
5 Bentinck Street, London W1M 5RN.

Contents

Introduction

Jane Austen was born in Steventon, Hampshire, in the south of England, in 1775. She was the seventh of eight children of George Austen, the minister of Steventon Church, and his wife Cassandra Leigh, whose father was also a church minister. Jane spent the first 25 years of her life at home in Steventon, where she learnt French, Italian, music and needlework. She was taught by her father, who encouraged her to read widely. The family also enjoyed performing plays, and it seems that Jane took part in these. She began writing at the age of fourteen as entertainment for her family.

When George Austen left his post in 1801, the family moved to Bath, a city which often features in Jane Austen's stories. When he died four years later, Jane moved back to Hampshire with her mother and sister and lived there until her death at the age of forty-one. The last few years of her life were affected by the development of the disease from which she died, and the suffering it caused her.

Jane Austen's life was an uneventful one, although some of her relatives led more exciting lives. She never married; she received proposals of marriage, though, and accepted one of them before changing her mind the next day. She was very close to her family, and in particular to her sister Cassandra, who also remained single. It seems that this quiet, ordered existence was necessary to Jane in order that she could write. She wrote very little while living in Bath, which was a relatively unsettled period in her life.

The restricted life that Jane Austen led had a strong influence on the subject matter of her stories, all of which deal with the everyday lives and concerns of middle-class people living in the countryside and towns of England. These people are anxious, above all, about their own and others' social position, about affairs of the heart and marriage. Austen's particular skill is the careful and humorous way in which she explores every detail of their lives. A strong sense of morality underlies her work, which makes it even more powerful. This moral sense is shown through Austen's description of her characters' behaviour; the writer's beliefs are not stated openly.

Austen's early writing often made gentle fun of popular fiction of the time. *Love and Friendship*, her first book (completed in 1790), was not very kind to those writers who scorned emotional self-control. *Northanger Abbey* was written at the same time, but only appeared after her death. The main character in this book reads a great deal, and as a result confuses literature with real life. *Sense and Sensibility* was begun in 1797 but did not appear in print until 1811. This book, *Pride and Prejudice* (1813), *Emma* (1816) and *Persuasion* (1817) are Austen's best-known works; they all deal in sharply and humorously observed detail with the manners and morals of one small social group. A more deeply serious work is *Mansfield Park* (1814); this has never been as popular with the reading public as the others, but to many it is the height of her achievement. Austen's novels were fairly popular in her lifetime, but it was only after her death that they achieved great success and that she was really given the respect she deserved.

Pride and Prejudice was originally written under the title *First Impressions*. Austen then rewrote the book as *Pride and Prejudice*, which appeared in 1813 and became probably the most popular of her works. Austen herself loved the book, calling it "my own darling child", and she was very fond of Elizabeth Bennet, the story's main character.

It was very important at that time for young women of a certain class to marry well, since they had no money or property of their own and were completely dependent on their fathers first and then on their husbands. The story shows how various characters choose their marriage partners, and the mistakes they make along the way. The underlying message is that it is not enough to marry for money alone; this will lead to unhappiness. Correct and polite behaviour is another important subject, but Austen shows that an honest and honourable nature is more important than social rules which are followed only on the surface.

Mrs Bennet's chief anxiety is her urgent need to find good husbands for all five of her daughters. So when a rich, unmarried young man rents a large house in the neighbourhood, her excitement reaches new heights; she is determined that Mr Bingley should marry one of the girls. He does in fact seem to be attracted to her oldest daughter, the calm and lovely Jane, but their relationship is not in fact an easy one. Mr Bingley has a rich friend named Darcy who begins to admire Jane's lively and amusing sister Elizabeth. On first sight, though, Elizabeth finds Mr Darcy much too proud and scornful of the company in which he finds himself, and she wants nothing to do with him. Gradually these four young people get to know each other, and themselves, much better, and they are often surprised by the discoveries they make.

Chapter 1   The Bennets

It is, of course, generally accepted that a wealthy single man must be in search of a wife. As soon as such a man moves into a neighbourhood, each of the families that live there will, without any inquiry as to his own feelings on the subject, immediately consider him the rightful property of one of their daughters.

'My dear Mr Bennet,' said Mrs Bennet to her husband one day, 'have you heard that Netherfield Park has been rented at last?'

Mr Bennet replied that he had not.

'But it has,' she repeated. 'Mrs Long has just been here, and she told me all about it.'

Mr Bennet made no answer.

'Do you not want to know who has taken it?' cried his wife impatiently.

'You want to tell me, and I have no objection to hearing it.'

This was quite enough encouragement.

'Well, my dear, Mrs Long says that Netherfield has been taken by a rich young man from the north of England, that he came down on Monday to see the place and was so pleased with it that he agreed to take possession immediately, and that some of his servants are to be in the house by the end of the week.'

'What is his name?'

'Bingley.'

'Is he married or single?'

'Oh, single, my dear! An unmarried man of large fortune – four or five thousand pounds a year. What a fine thing for our girls!'

'And why is that? What difference does it make to them?'

'My dear Mr Bennet,' replied his wife, 'how can you be so

annoying? You must know that I am thinking of his marrying one of them.'

'Is that his intention in settling here?'

'Intention? Nonsense, how can you talk like that! But it is likely that he may fall in love with one of them, and therefore you must visit him as soon as he comes.'

'I see no reason for that. You and the girls may go, or, even better, you may send them by themselves, because as you are as good-looking as any of them, Mr Bingley might like you the best of the party.'

'My dear, you praise me too highly. I certainly *have* had my share of beauty, but when a woman has five grown-up daughters, she ought to give up thinking of her own appearance. But you must go and see Mr Bingley when he comes.'

'I cannot promise to do so.'

'But consider your daughters. You must go, because it will be impossible for us to visit him if you do not.'

'You are too anxious to do what is proper, surely. I dare say Mr Bingley will be very glad to see you, and I will send him a few words by you to inform him of my complete agreement to his marrying whichever of the girls he chooses, though I must throw in a good word for my little Lizzy.'

'I hope you will do no such thing. Lizzy is not a bit better than the others, but you are always showing a preference for her.'

'They have none of them much about them to admire,' he replied. 'They are all silly and empty-headed like other girls, but Lizzy is a little more intelligent than her sisters.'

'Mr Bennet, how can you speak of your own daughters in such a way? You take pleasure in annoying me. You have no pity on my poor nerves.'

'You are mistaken, my dear. I have a high respect for your nerves. They are my old friends. I have been listening to news of them for the last 20 years.'

'Ah! You do not know how I suffer.'

Mr Bennet was such a strange mixture of cleverness, sharp humour, silence and unexpected changes of mind, that the experience of 23 years had not been long enough to make his wife understand his character. Her mind was less difficult to understand. She was a foolish woman. When she was anxious, she imagined herself to be ill. The business of her life was to get her daughters married; its pleasure was visiting and news.

Chapter 2   New Neighbours at Netherfield

Mr Bennet was among the first of those who visited Mr Bingley. He had always intended to do so, though he continued to let his wife believe that he would not go. He finally made his intentions known in the following way.

Watching his second daughter occupied in sewing a coloured band around a hat, he suddenly addressed her with:

'I hope Mr Bingley will like it, Lizzy.'

'We are not in a position to know *what* Mr Bingley likes,' said her mother bitterly, 'if we are not to visit him.'

'But you forget, mother,' said Elizabeth, 'that we shall meet him at the public balls, and that Mrs Long has promised to introduce him.'

'I do not believe Mrs Long will do any such thing. She has two nieces of her own. She is a selfish, insincere woman, and I have no opinion of her.'

'Neither have I,' said Mr Bennet, 'and I am glad to find that you do not depend on her serving you.'

Mrs Bennet would not make any reply, but, unable to control her annoyance, began complaining to one of her daughters.

'Don't keep coughing so, Kitty! Have a little pity on my poor nerves.'

'Kitty lacks judgment in her coughs,' said her father. 'She chooses the wrong moment.'

'I do not cough for my own amusement,' replied Kitty. 'When is your next ball to be, Lizzy?'

'In two weeks from tomorrow.'

'So it is,' cried her mother, 'and Mrs Long does not come back until the day before, so it will be impossible for her to introduce him, because she will not know him herself.'

'Then, my dear, you may have the advantage of your friend, and introduce Mr Bingley to *her*.'

'Impossible, Mr Bennet, impossible, when I am not acquainted with him myself. How can you be so annoying!'

'Well, if you will not perform this duty, I will do it myself.'

The girls looked at their father. Mrs Bennet said: 'Nonsense, nonsense! I am sick of Mr Bingley.'

'I am sorry to hear that, but why did you not tell me so before? If I had known it this morning, I certainly would not have gone to see him. It is very unlucky, but as I have actually paid the visit, we cannot escape the acquaintance now.'

The astonishment of the ladies was just what he wished, that of Mrs Bennet being perhaps beyond the rest, though when the first excitement was over, she began to say that it was what she had expected all the time.

'How good it was of you! I was sure you loved your girls too well to neglect such an acquaintance. Well, how pleased I am! And it is such a good joke, too, that you went this morning, and never said a word about it until now.'

'Now, Kitty, you may cough as much as you choose,' said Mr Bennet, as he left the room, having had enough of his wife's talk.

'What an excellent father you have, girls,' she said, when the door was shut. 'I do not know how you will ever repay him for his kindness. At our time of life, it is not so pleasant, I can tell you, to be making new acquaintances every day, but for our dear daughters we would do anything. Lydia, my love, though you are the youngest, I dare say Mr Bingley will dance with you at the next ball.'

'Oh,' said Lydia confidently, 'I am not afraid. Though I am the youngest, I'm the tallest.'

The rest of the evening was spent discussing how soon Mr Bingley would return Mr Bennet's visit, and deciding when they should ask him to dinner.

♦

All that Mrs Bennet, together with her five daughters, could ask on the subject, was not enough to draw from her husband any satisfactory description of Mr Bingley. They were forced at last to accept the second-hand information of their neighbour, Lady Lucas. Her report was highly favourable. He was quite young, very good-looking, extremely agreeable, and, in addition to all this, he planned to be at the next public ball. Nothing could be more exciting!

In a few days Mr Bingley returned Mr Bennet's visit, and sat for about ten minutes with him in the library. He had hoped to see the young ladies, of whose beauty he had heard a great deal, but he saw only the father. The ladies were more fortunate. They had the advantage of observing, from an upstairs window, that he wore a blue coat and rode a black horse.

An invitation to dinner was sent soon after, and Mrs Bennet had already planned the meal that was to show the quality of her housekeeping, when an answer arrived which changed everything. Mr Bingley found it necessary to be in London the following day, and was therefore unable to accept the honour of their invitation. Mrs Bennet was both disappointed and worried. She began to fear that he might always be flying about from one place to another, and never settled in Netherfield as he ought to be. Lady Lucas quietened her fears a little by spreading the word that he had gone to London only to collect a large party for the ball, and a report soon followed that Mr Bingley would bring twelve ladies and seven gentlemen with him. The girls were unhappy at the thought of such a large number of ladies, but were comforted to find, when the party entered the ballroom, that it was in fact made up of only five altogether: Mr Bingley, his two sisters, the husband of the older one, and another young man.

Mr Bingley was good-looking and gentlemanly. His sisters were fine women dressed in the latest fashions. His sister's husband, Mr Hurst, simply looked like the gentleman he was, but Mr Darcy soon drew the attention of everyone by his fine tall form, noble face, and the report, which was passed round the room within five minutes of his entrance, that he had an income of ten thousand pounds a year. He was looked at with admiration for half the evening, until his manners caused a general disgust which ended his popularity.

Mr Bingley had soon made himself acquainted with all the important people in the room. He danced every dance, was angry that the ball closed so early, and talked of giving one himself at Netherfield. What a difference between himself and his friend! Mr Darcy danced only once with Mrs Hurst and once with Miss Bingley, refused to be introduced to any other lady, and spent the rest of the evening walking around the room. Mrs Bennet's dislike of his behaviour was sharpened by his having made one of her daughters appear neglected.

Elizabeth Bennet had been forced, by the small number of gentlemen, to sit out for two dances, and during part of that time Mr Darcy had been standing near enough for her to hear, against her will, a conversation between him and Mr Bingley, who left the dancing for a few minutes to urge his friend to join in.

'Come, Darcy,' he said, 'I hate to see you standing around by yourself like this. You really should be dancing.'

'I certainly shall not. Both your sisters already have partners, and there is not another woman in the room with whom I would care to dance.'

'I would not like to be so difficult to please as you are,' cried Bingley. 'I have never met with so many pleasant girls in my life.'

'You are dancing with the only good-looking one,' said Mr Darcy, looking at the oldest Miss Bennet.

'Oh, she is the most beautiful creature that I ever saw! But there is one of her sisters sitting down just behind you, who is very attractive and probably very agreeable. Do let me ask my partner to introduce you.'

'Which do you mean?' Darcy asked. Turning round, he looked for a moment at Elizabeth, until, catching her eye, he looked away and coldly said: 'She is fairly pretty, but not good-looking enough.'

He walked off, and Elizabeth remained with no very friendly feelings towards him. But she told the story with great spirit among her friends, because she had a playful nature and a strong sense of humour.

The evening on the whole passed off pleasantly for all the family. Mrs Bennet had seen her oldest daughter much admired by the Netherfield party. Mr Bingley had danced with her twice, and she had been an object of attention by his sisters. Jane was as much pleased by this as her mother, though in a quieter way. Elizabeth shared Jane's pleasure, as she always did. Lydia and Kitty had never been without partners, and Mary, the least pretty of the family, had heard herself praised to Miss Bingley as a skilled musician.

They returned, therefore, in good spirits to Longbourn, the village in Hertfordshire where they lived, and of which they were the most important family.

♦

Within a short walk of Longbourn there lived a family with whom the Bennets were especially friendly. Sir William Lucas had formerly been in trade in the town of Meryton, where he had made a fairly large fortune and risen to the honour of a title of rank. This honour had, perhaps, been felt too strongly. It had given him a disgust for his business and for his home in a small market town, and, leaving them both, he had moved with his family to a house about a mile from Meryton, which he called Lucas Lodge. But though proud of his rank, he was friendly and ready to help anyone who needed it. Lady Lucas was a very good kind of woman, not too clever to be a valuable neighbour to Mrs Bennet. They had several children. The oldest of them, a sensible young woman of about twenty-seven, was Elizabeth's special friend.

It was a time-honoured tradition for the Misses Lucas and the Misses Bennet to meet and talk after a ball, and so the following morning brought the former to Longbourn for that purpose.

'You began the evening well, Charlotte,' said Mrs Bennet, with forced politeness, to Miss Lucas. 'You were Mr Bingley's first choice.'

'Yes, but he seemed to like his second better.'

'Oh, you mean Jane, I suppose, because he danced with her twice. Certainly that did seem as if he admired her. It *does* seem as if – but it may not lead to anything, you know.'

'But Mr Darcy is not so worth listening to as his friend, is he?' said Charlotte. 'Poor Eliza! To be only just *fairly* pretty!'

'I hope you will not put it into Lizzy's head to be annoyed by his rude treatment. He is such a disagreeable man that it would be quite a misfortune to be liked by him. Mrs Long told me last night that he sat next to her for half an hour without once opening his lips.'

'Are you quite sure, madam? Is there not some mistake?' said Jane. 'I certainly saw Mr Darcy speaking to her.'

'Yes, because she finally asked him how he liked Netherfield, and he could not help answering her, but she said he seemed very angry at being spoken to.'

'Miss Bingley told me,' said Jane, 'that he never speaks much except among people he knows well. With them he is extremely agreeable.'

'I do not believe a word of it, my dear.'

'I do not mind his not talking to Mrs Long,' said Miss Lucas, 'but I wish he had danced with Eliza.'

'Another time, Lizzy,' said her mother, 'I would not dance with him, if I were you.'

'His pride,' said Miss Lucas, 'does not offend me so much as pride often does, because there is an excuse for it. One cannot be surprised that such a fine young man with family and fortune should think highly of himself.'

'That is very true,' replied Eliza, 'and I could easily forgive his pride, if he had not wounded *mine*.'

Chapter 3   Jane Gains an Admirer

The ladies of Longbourn soon visited those of Netherfield. The visit was formally returned. Miss Bennet's pleasing manners continued to win the approval of Mrs Hurst and Miss Bingley, and though the mother was considered to be unbearable, and the younger sisters not worth speaking to, a wish was expressed to be better acquainted with the two oldest. This attention was received by Jane with the greatest pleasure, but Elizabeth saw pride in their treatment of everybody, even her sister, and could not like them. But it was plain that their brother *did* admire Jane, and Elizabeth observed that Jane was giving way to the preference which she had begun to feel for him from the first, and was beginning to be very much in love.

While Elizabeth was watching Mr Bingley's attentions to her sister, she did not realize that she herself was becoming an object of some interest in the eyes of his friend. Mr Darcy had at first hardly admitted her to be pretty; he had seen her without admiration at the ball, and when they next met, he looked at her only to criticize. But he had no sooner decided that no single part of her face was particularly attractive than he began to find that the whole was made uncommonly intelligent by the beautiful expression of her dark eyes. She was completely unconscious of this. To her, he was only the man who had made himself agreeable nowhere, and who had not thought her attractive enough to dance with.

He began to wish to know her better.

One day, a large party was amusing itself at Sir William Lucas's. A number of young ladies, and two or three army officers, were occupied in dancing at one end of the room. Mr Darcy stood near them, and Sir William was trying to make conversation with him. As Elizabeth moved towards them at this moment, Sir William was struck with the idea of doing the polite thing, and called out to her:

'My dear Miss Eliza, why are you not dancing? Mr Darcy, you must allow me to present this young lady to you as a very desirable partner. You cannot refuse to dance, I am sure, when so much beauty is in front of you.' And, taking her hand, he would have given it to Mr Darcy, who, though extremely surprised, was not unwilling to receive it, when she immediately pulled away, and said in some confusion to Sir William:

'Sir, I have not the least intention of dancing. Please do not suppose that I moved this way in order to beg for a partner.'

Mr Darcy, with great politeness, requested to be allowed the honour of her hand, but without success. Elizabeth was determined, and Sir William's attempt at persuasion met with no success.

'You are such an excellent dancer, Miss Eliza, that it is cruel to refuse me the happiness of seeing you, and though this gentleman dislikes the amusement in general, he can have no objection, I am sure, to doing us this honour for one half-hour.'

'Mr Darcy is all politeness,' said Elizabeth smiling. She turned away. Her refusal had not harmed her in the gentleman's opinion, and he thought of her with some admiration.

♦

The village of Longbourn was only one mile from the town of Meryton – a most convenient distance for the young ladies, who usually went there three or four times a week to make a visit to an aunt, Mrs Philips, who was married to a lawyer, and to look at a hat shop just over the way. The two youngest of the family, Catherine and Lydia, were particularly frequent in these attentions. They always managed to learn some news, and at present they were well supplied by the arrival of a regiment in the neighbourhood, which would remain for the whole winter. They could talk of nothing but officers.

After listening one morning to their excited remarks on this subject, Mr Bennet sharply observed:

'From all that I can understand from your manner of talking, you must be two of the silliest girls in the country.'

Kitty was a little ashamed, and did not answer, but Lydia laughed loudly.

'I am astonished, my dear,' said Mrs Bennet, 'that you should be so ready to think your own children silly. As a matter of fact, they are all very clever.'

'This is the only point on which we do not agree.'

Mrs Bennet was prevented from replying by the entrance of a servant with a note for Miss Bennet. It came from Netherfield. Mrs Bennet's eyes brightened with pleasure, and she called out eagerly, while her daughter read:

'Well, Jane, who is it from? What is it about? What does he say? Well, Jane, hurry up and tell us.'

'It is from Miss Bingley,' said Jane, and then read it aloud:

NETHERFIELD PARK
10th October

My dear Jane,

Will you be so kind as to come to dinner today with Louisa and me? We are all alone. Come as soon as you can on receiving this. My brother and the gentlemen are to have dinner with the officers.

Yours ever,

CAROLINE BINGLEY.

'Having dinner out,' said Mrs Bennet, 'that is very unlucky.'

'Can I have the carriage?' asked Jane.

'No, my dear, you had better go on horseback, because it seems likely to rain and then you must stay all night.'

'That would be a good idea,' said Elizabeth, 'if you were sure that they would not offer to send her home.'

'Oh, but the gentlemen will have used Mr Bingley's carriage to go to Meryton.'

'I would much rather go in the carriage,' repeated Jane.

'But, my dear, your father does not have enough horses. They are wanted on the farm.'

Jane was therefore forced to go on horseback, and her mother followed her to the door with many cheerful wishes for bad weather. Her hopes were answered. Jane had not been gone long before it rained hard. Her sisters were anxious for her, but her mother was pleased. The rain continued the whole evening. Jane certainly could not come back.

'This was a good idea of mine!' said Mrs Bennet.

Breakfast was hardly over next morning when a servant from

Netherfield brought a note for Elizabeth from Jane to say that she was unwell.

'Well, my dear,' said Mr Bennet, when Elizabeth had read the note out loud, 'if your daughter should have a dangerous attack of illness – if she should die – it will be a comfort to know that it was all the result of going after Mr Bingley, and following your orders.'

'Oh, I am not afraid of her dying. People do not die of little things like colds. They will take good care of her.'

Elizabeth, feeling really anxious, decided to go to her sister. The carriage was not available, and as she did not ride a horse, walking was her only possible way.

'How can you be so silly,' said her mother, 'in all this mud! You will not be fit to be seen when you get there.'

'I shall be very fit to see Jane, which is all I want.'

'We will go as far as Meryton with you,' offered Lydia and Kitty. Elizabeth accepted their company, and the three young ladies set off together.

At Meryton they parted, and Elizabeth continued her walk alone, crossing field after field impatiently, and finding herself at last within sight of the house, with tired feet, dirty shoes, and a face bright with the warmth of exercise.

Her appearance caused a great deal of surprise. Elizabeth guessed that Mrs Hurst and Miss Bingley were scornful that she should walk 3 miles so early and in such weather. She was received, though, very politely, and in their brother's manner was something better than politeness – kindness and pleasure. Mr Darcy said very little. He was occupied with admiring the brightness that exercise had added to the colour in her face.

Her sister Jane had hardly slept at all, and was feverish. The doctor came, advised her to return to bed, and promised some medicine. The fever increased, and her head ached badly.

Elizabeth stayed with her until three o'clock, and then felt she must go. But Jane showed such disappointment at parting from her that Miss Bingley was forced to invite her to remain at Netherfield for the present, and Elizabeth thankfully accepted this offer. A servant was sent to Longbourn to tell the family of her stay and to bring back a supply of clothes.

♦

At half past six, Elizabeth was called to dinner. Jane was not at all better. Mr Bingley's sisters, on hearing this, repeated three or four times how sorry they were, how unpleasant it was to have a bad cold, and how very much they disliked being ill themselves, and then thought no more of the matter. Their lack of real feeling towards Jane, when she was not actually in their presence, brought back to Elizabeth all her original dislike of them.

Their brother was in fact the only one whose anxiety for Jane seemed sincere. His attentions to Elizabeth herself were most pleasing, and they prevented her from feeling herself such an unwelcome guest as she believed she was considered to be by the others.

When dinner was over, she returned directly to Jane, and Miss Bingley began criticizing her as soon as she was out of the room. How poor her manners were – a mixture of pride and lack of good family. She had no powers of conversation, no style, no taste, no beauty. Mrs Hurst thought the same, and added:

'There is nothing to admire in her except being an excellent walker. I shall never forget her appearance this morning. She really looked almost wild.'

'She certainly did, Louisa. Her hair so untidy!'

'Yes, and her skirt! I hope you saw her skirt, covered in mud.'

'I thought Miss Elizabeth Bennet looked extremely well when she came into the room this morning,' said Mr Bingley. 'Her dirty skirt quite escaped my notice. Her coming shows a concern for her sister that is very pleasing.'

'I am afraid, Mr Darcy,' observed Miss Bingley, in a half-whisper, 'that this adventure has rather lessened your admiration for her fine eyes.'

'Not at all,' he replied. 'They were brightened by the exercise.'

A short pause followed this speech, and Mrs Hurst began again:

'I am extremely fond of Jane Bennet. She is really a very sweet girl. I wish with all my heart that she were well settled. But with such parents, and such low relations, I am afraid there is no chance of it.'

'It must greatly lessen her chance of marrying a man of good position,' replied Mr Darcy.

Mr Bingley made no answer to this speech, but his sisters gave it their full agreement, and continued for some time to make fun of their dear friend's inferior relations.

◆

Elizabeth spent most of the night in her sister's room, and in the morning requested that a note be sent to Longbourn, asking her mother to visit Jane and form her own judgment on her condition. The note was immediately sent, and Mrs Bennet, with her two youngest girls, reached Netherfield soon after breakfast.

If Mrs Bennet had found Jane in any real danger, she would have been very upset, but when she was satisfied that her illness was not serious, she had no wish for her immediate recovery, as her return to health would probably remove her from Netherfield. She would not listen, therefore, to her daughter's proposal of being taken home; nor did the doctor, who arrived at about the same time, think it advisable.

Mrs Bennet repeated her thanks to Mr Bingley for his kindness to Jane, with an apology for troubling him also with Lizzy. Mr Bingley was eager that his two guests should remain, and forced his younger sister to be polite too. She did this duty, even if rather unwillingly, but Mrs Bennet was satisfied, and left soon after that.

The day passed much as the day before had done. Jane was slowly recovering. In the evening, Elizabeth joined the company in the sitting room, and took up some needlework. Mr Darcy was writing a letter.

When that business was over, he asked Miss Bingley and Elizabeth to play some music. Miss Bingley moved eagerly to the piano. After a polite request for Elizabeth to begin the performance, which Elizabeth refused with equal politeness, Miss Bingley seated herself.

Mrs Hurst sang with her sister; and while they were employed in this, Elizabeth could not help noticing how frequently Mr Darcy's eyes fixed themselves on her. She could hardly imagine that she could be an object of admiration to so great a man, but it seemed even stranger that he should look at her so, because she knew he disliked her. She could only suppose that she drew his attention because there was something wrong about her. The supposition did not upset her; she liked him too little to care for his opinion.

Soon after, as Miss Bingley began to play a lively Scottish tune, Mr Darcy, approaching Elizabeth, said to her:

'Do you not feel a great desire, Miss Bennet, to seize such an opportunity for a dance?'

She smiled, but made no answer. He repeated the question, with some surprise at her silence.

'Oh,' she said, 'I heard you before, but I could not decide immediately on what to say in reply. You wanted me, I know, to say "Yes", so that you might have the pleasure of thinking badly of my taste, but I always enjoy defeating such intentions. I have, therefore, made up my mind to tell you that I do not want to dance; and now, think badly of me if you dare.'

'I do not dare.'

Elizabeth, having rather expected to offend him, was astonished at his politeness, but there was a mixture of sweetness and intelligence in her manner that made it difficult for her to offend anybody. Darcy had never been so attracted to any woman as he was to her. He really believed that, if it were not for her inferior relations, he would be in some danger of falling in love.

Miss Bingley saw, or thought she saw, enough to be jealous, and her anxiety for the recovery of her dear friend Jane was increased by her desire to get rid of Elizabeth.

As a result of an agreement between the two sisters, Elizabeth wrote the next morning to her mother to beg her to send the carriage for them during that day. Mrs Bennet sent them a reply that they could not possibly have it before Tuesday. But Elizabeth had decided that she could stay no longer, nor did she very much expect that she would be encouraged to. She urged Jane to borrow Mr Bingley's carriage immediately.

The master of the house heard with real sorrow that they were leaving so soon, and repeatedly tried to persuade the older Miss Bennet that it was not safe for her, but Jane was always able to be decisive when she believed herself to be right.

It was welcome news to Mr Darcy. Elizabeth attracted him more than he wished. He decided to be particularly careful that no sign of admiration should now escape him. He kept steadily to his purpose, and hardly spoke to her through the whole of the day, and although they were at one time left by themselves for half an hour, he kept firmly to his book and would not even look at her.

On the next morning, they left for home. They were not welcomed back very gladly by their mother, but their father was really happy to see them. The evening conversation had lost much of its liveliness, and most of its good sense, during the absence of Jane and Elizabeth.

Chapter 4   Mr Collins

'I hope, my dear,' said Mr Bennet to his wife, as they were at breakfast the next morning, 'that you have ordered a good dinner today, because I have reason to expect an addition to our family party.'

'Whom do you mean, my dear? I know of nobody that is coming, I am sure, unless Charlotte Lucas should happen to call, and I hope my dinners are good enough for *her*.'

'The person of whom I speak is a gentleman and a stranger.'

Mrs Bennet's eyes brightened. 'A gentleman and a stranger! It is Mr Bingley, I am sure! Why, Jane, you never mentioned a word about this! But – good heavens! How unlucky! There is not a bit of fish to be got today! Lydia, my love, ring the bell. I must speak to the cook immediately.'

'It is *not* Mr Bingley,' said her husband. 'It is a person whom I have never seen in the whole of my life.'

This caused general astonishment, and he had the pleasure of being eagerly questioned by his wife and all five of his daughters at once.

After amusing himself for some time by not answering their questions, he explained:

'A short time ago I received a letter. It was from my cousin, Mr Collins, who, when I am dead, may put you all out of this house as soon as he pleases.'

Mr Bennet's property was, unfortunately for his daughters, to pass by law after his death to his nearest male relative, a distant cousin.

'Oh, my dear,' cried his wife, 'I cannot bear to hear that mentioned. Please do not talk of that hateful man.' It was a subject on which she could never see reason.

'But if you will listen to his letter, you may perhaps be a little softened by his manner of expressing himself:

15th October

Dear Sir,

The disagreement that existed between yourself and my honoured father always caused me much anxiety, and since his death I have frequently wished for a renewal of friendship between our two branches of the family.

My mind is now made up on the subject. I have recently become a minister of the church and I have been fortunate enough to become the object of attention of the Lady Catherine de Bourgh. By her generosity I have been presented with a valuable position in this area, where I shall try to behave with grateful respect towards her.

As a churchman, I feel it to be my duty to encourage peace among all families within my influence, and for these reasons I consider that my offer of friendship is deserving of praise, and that the fact that I am heir to your property will be kindly forgiven by you.

I am troubled at being the means of harming your daughters, and beg to apologize for it, as well as to inform you of my readiness to do what is in my power to lessen the wrong done to them.

If you have no objection to receiving me into your house, I intend to visit you and your family on Monday next week, at four o'clock, and would be thankful to remain as your guest until the Saturday of the following week.

I remain, dear sir, with respectful greetings to your lady and daughters, your well-wisher and friend,

WILLIAM COLLINS.

'At four o'clock, therefore, we may expect this peace-making gentleman,' said Mr Bennet, as he folded up the letter. 'He seems a most dutiful and polite young man.'

'There is some sense in what he says about trying to lessen the harm done to the girls,' his wife agreed.

'Though it is difficult,' said Jane, 'to guess in what way he intends to do so.'

Elizabeth was chiefly struck with his high degree of respect for Lady Catherine. As for her mother, Mr Collins's letter had taken away much of her unfriendly feeling, and she prepared herself to see him with a calmness that astonished her husband and daughters.

♦

Mr Collins arrived on time, and was received with great politeness by the whole family. Mr Bennet said little, but the ladies were ready enough to talk, and Mr Collins seemed very willing to do so himself. He was a tall, heavy-looking young man of about twenty-five. His manner was serious and his behaviour very formal. He had not been seated long before he began to offer his congratulations to Mrs Bennet on having such a fine family of daughters, and to admire their beauty. He added that he did not doubt that she would in time see them all well settled in marriage. This speech was not much to the taste of some of his hearers, but Mrs Bennet answered most readily:

'You are very kind, sir, I am sure, and I wish with all my heart that it may be so, or they will be poor enough. These matters are settled in such a strange way.'

'I am conscious, madam, of the injustice to your lovely daughters, but they may be sure that I have come prepared to admire them. At present I will say no more, but perhaps, when we are better acquainted . . .'

He was interrupted by the announcement of dinner, and the girls smiled at each other. They were not the only objects of Mr Collins's admiration. The hall, the dining room, and all its furniture, were examined and highly praised, and his approval would have touched Mrs Bennet's heart, if she had not believed that he was viewing it all as his own future property. The dinner, too, in its turn, was much admired, and he begged to know which of his cousins had prepared the excellent meal. But here he was corrected by Mrs Bennet, who informed him rather sharply that they could very well afford to keep a good cook, and that her daughters had nothing to do in the kitchen. He begged pardon for having displeased her. She replied in a softer voice that she was not at all offended, but he continued to apologize for about a quarter of an hour.

After dinner, Mr Bennet thought it was time to have some conversation with his guest. He therefore chose a subject on which he expected Mr Collins would be pleased to speak, and began by observing that he seemed very fortunate in receiving such an excellent living from Lady Catherine. Mr Bennet could not have thought of a better beginning. Mr Collins praised her loudly, expressing himself in an extremely respectful manner. By teatime his host had had enough, and was glad to take the young man into the sitting room and invite him to read to the ladies. Mr Collins readily agreed, and a book was produced, but at the sight of it he quickly stated, begging pardon, that he never read works of fiction. Kitty and Lydia looked at him in surprise. Other books were offered, and he chose a collection of writings on matters of religion. Lydia turned away as he opened the book, and before he had, in a dull voice, read three pages, she interrupted to speak to her mother. Her two oldest sisters urged her to hold her tongue, but Mr Collins, much offended, laid the book down.

◆

Mr Collins was not a sensible man, and neither education nor society had improved him much. He was too conscious of his own importance, and, at the same time, too afraid of giving offence, especially to those above him in rank.

A fortunate chance had brought him to the attention of Lady Catherine de Bourgh, when the position at Hunsford became free. Having now a good house and a large enough income, he intended to marry. In ending the quarrel with the Longbourn family, he was thinking of a wife, as he meant to choose one of the daughters. This was his plan of lessening the wrong done to them by his being the heir to their father's property, and he thought it was an extremely generous one.

His plan did not change on seeing them. Miss Jane Bennet's beautiful face soon attracted him, and for the first evening *she* was his settled choice. But the next morning caused a change, because in a quarter of an hour's private talk with Mrs Bennet before breakfast, he received a warning about the cousin whom he had fixed on. 'As to her *younger* daughters, she could not be sure, she could not answer immediately – but her *oldest* daughter, she must just mention, she felt it her duty to state, was likely to be very soon engaged to be married.'

Mr Collins had only to change from Jane to Elizabeth. It was done in a moment. Elizabeth, next to Jane both in birth and beauty, followed her as his choice as a matter of course.

Mrs Bennet was pleased with this suggestion, and trusted that she might soon have two daughters married. The man whom she could not bear to speak of the day before now stood high in her regard.

Chapter 5   Mr Wickham

Lydia intended to walk to Meryton that morning, and every sister except Mary, who preferred to read, agreed to go with her. Mr Collins was their companion, at the request of Mr Bennet, who was most anxious to get rid of him and have his library to himself because his cousin never stopped talking.

The girls listened politely to his remarks until they entered Meryton. The attention of the younger ones was then no longer to be won by *him*. Their eyes were immediately wandering up the street in search of the officers.

But the attention of every lady was soon caught by a young man whom they had never seen before. He was of a most gentlemanly appearance and was walking with an officer on the other side of the road. All were struck by the stranger's manner. Kitty and Lydia knew the officer, and decided to find out who his friend was. They led the way across the street, under pretence of wanting something in a shop opposite, and had just reached the pathway when the two gentlemen arrived at the same place. Mr Denny, the officer, addressed them directly and introduced his friend, Mr Wickham, who had just joined the army.

The young man appeared very pleasant. He was good-looking and he had a fine figure and very pleasing manners. The whole party was still having a pleasant conversation, when the sound of horses drew their attention, and Darcy and Bingley were seen riding down the street. On recognizing the ladies in the group, the two gentlemen came directly towards them, and began the usual polite greetings. Bingley was the chief speaker, and Miss Jane Bennet the chief object. He was then, he said, on his way to Longbourn to inquire after her health. Mr Darcy followed him, and was beginning to decide to keep his eyes away from Elizabeth, when they suddenly became fixed on the stranger. Elizabeth happened to see the faces of both when they looked at each other, and was astonished at the effect of the meeting. The face of one became white, the other turned red. Mr Wickham, after a few moments, touched his hat in greeting, but Mr Darcy seemed hardly to move a finger in return. What could be the meaning of it? It was impossible to imagine, and it was impossible not to want to know the reason for this behaviour.

In another minute, Mr Bingley, who seemed not to have noticed what had happened, said goodbye to the ladies and rode on with his friend.

As they walked home, Elizabeth described to Jane what she had seen pass between the two gentlemen, but Jane could no more explain such behaviour than her sister.

♦

At Meryton the young people had accepted an invitation from their aunt to supper and cards. The carriage took Mr Collins and his five cousins at a suitable hour to the town, and the girls had the pleasure of hearing, as they entered the sitting room, that Mr Wickham had accepted an invitation from their uncle to be present, and was already in the house.

When this information was given, and they had all taken their seats, Mr Collins was free to look around him and talk. To the girls the time of waiting appeared very long, but it was over at last. The gentlemen joined them, and when Mr Wickham walked into the room, Elizabeth felt that she had not been thinking of him with at all unreasonable admiration.

Mr Wickham was the happy man towards whom almost every lady's eye was turned, and Elizabeth was the happy woman by whom he seated himself at last. With such fine men as Mr Wickham and the officers in competition for the attention of the ladies, Mr Collins seemed to sink into unimportance, but he still had from time to time a kind listener in Mrs Philips.

Elizabeth was very willing to hear Mr Wickham talk, though she could not hope to be told what she chiefly wished to hear – the history of his acquaintance with Mr Darcy. But her interest was most unexpectedly satisfied. Mr Wickham began the subject himself. He asked slowly how long Mr Darcy had been staying in the area.

'About a month,' said Elizabeth, and then, unwilling to let the subject drop, she added: 'He is a man of very large property in Derbyshire, I believe.'

'Yes,' replied Wickham, 'Pemberley, his property there, is a noble one – at least ten thousand a year. You could not have met with a person better able to give you information about it than myself. I have been connected with his family since my birth.'

Elizabeth could not help looking surprised.

'You may well be surprised, Miss Bennet, at such a statement, after seeing the very cold manner of our meeting yesterday. Do you know Mr Darcy well?'

'Quite as well as I ever wish to do,' cried Elizabeth warmly. 'I have spent several days in the same house with him, and I find him very disagreeable.'

'I cannot pretend to be sorry,' said Wickham, after a short pause. 'His behaviour to me has been shameful. I could have forgiven him anything, though, except for his disappointing the hopes of his father and bringing shame on his memory.'

Elizabeth's interest in the subject increased.

'I was educated for the Church,' continued Mr Wickham, 'and Mr Darcy's father left me, on his death, the best living to which he had the power to make an appointment, as soon as it became free. He was my godfather and he was very fond of me. He thought that he had provided for my future, but the living was given to somebody else.'

'Good heavens!' said Elizabeth. 'But surely that was against the law?'

'My godfather's wishes were not expressed clearly. Mr Darcy treated his father's words as a suggestion with certain conditions connected with it, and claimed that I had no right to the living because of some imagined wrongdoings of mine. But the fact is that he hates me.'

'This is quite shameful! He deserves that the truth should be made public.'

'Until I can forget his father, I can never be the means of shaming the son.'

Elizabeth honoured him for such feelings.

'We were born in the same place, and brought up together. My father managed the late Mr Darcy's affairs, and gave all his time to the care of his property.'

'I am surprised that Mr Darcy's pride has not made him fairer to you. I should have thought that he would have been too proud to be dishonest.'

'It is surprising,' replied Wickham, 'because his pride has often caused him to be generous, to give his money freely, to be an excellent host and a kind landowner, and to do good to the poor. He also has brotherly pride. He looks after his sister very well.'

'What sort of a girl is Miss Darcy?'

He shook his head. 'I wish I could call her likeable. But she is too much like her brother – very, very proud.'

'I am astonished at Mr Darcy's friendship with Mr Bingley. How can Mr Bingley, who is so agreeable and friendly to everyone, like such a man? He cannot know what Mr Darcy is.'

'Probably not. But Mr Darcy can please when he wishes. He can be a good companion if he thinks it worth taking the trouble. He is a very different man among those who are his equals in the world.'

Mr Wickham's attention was caught a little later by Mr Collins mentioning the name of Lady Catherine de Bourgh. He asked Elizabeth in a low voice whether her relations were acquainted with the family.

'You know, of course, that Lady Catherine de Bourgh and Lady Anne Darcy were sisters, and therefore she is aunt to the present Mr Darcy. Her daughter, Miss de Bourgh, will have a very large fortune, and it is believed that she and her cousin will unite the two properties by marriage.'

This information made Elizabeth smile, as she thought of Miss Bingley. All that lady's hopes would be disappointed, if he was already promised to another.

Chapter 6   The Ball at Netherfield

Elizabeth repeated to Jane, the next day, what had passed between Mr Wickham and herself. Jane listened with astonishment and concern. She could not believe that Mr Darcy could be so undeserving of Mr Bingley's friendship, but it was not in her nature to question the truthfulness of a young man of such pleasing appearance as Wickham.

'They have both been mistaken, I expect,' she said, 'in some way or other, of which we can form no idea.'

The two young ladies were called from the garden, where this conversation was taking place, by the arrival of some of the persons of whom they had been speaking. Mr Bingley and his sisters came to give their personal invitation for the long-expected ball at Netherfield, which was fixed for the following Tuesday. Miss Bingley and Mrs Hurst appeared very pleased to see their dear friend again, and complained that it was a long time since they had last met. They took very little notice of the rest of the family, avoiding Mrs Bennet as much as possible, saying not much to Elizabeth, and nothing at all to the others.

The thought of the Netherfield ball was exciting to every female of the family. Mrs Bennet considered it to be given as a mark of attention to her oldest daughter, and was particularly pleased at receiving the invitation from Mr Bingley himself, instead of by means of a formal card. Jane pictured to herself a happy evening in the society of her two friends and the attentions of their brother, and Elizabeth thought with pleasure of dancing a great deal with Mr Wickham. The happiness of Kitty and Lydia depended less on any special event or person. All that they wished for was plenty of partners. Even the serious-minded Mary was willing to go.

Elizabeth's spirits were so high that though she did not often speak unnecessarily to Mr Collins, she could not help asking him whether he intended to accept Mr Bingley's invitation. To her surprise, he replied that he would go, and added:

'I shall hope to be honoured in the dance with the hands of all my cousins in the course of the evening, and I take this opportunity of asking for yours, Miss Elizabeth, for the first two dances especially. I trust that my cousin Jane will understand the reasons for this preference, and not think that it is in any way disrespectful to her.'

Elizabeth felt herself completely at a disadvantage. She had fully intended being promised to Wickham for those same dances, and to have Mr Collins instead! Her liveliness had never been expressed at a worse moment. But she could do nothing. Mr Collins's offer was accepted with as much pleasure as she could manage to show. It now first struck her, though, that *she* was chosen from among her sisters as being suitable in his opinion to be his wife at Hunsford Parsonage. The idea was soon strengthened as she observed his increasing politeness to her, and though she herself was more astonished than pleased, it was not long before her mother let her know that the possibility of their marriage was extremely pleasing to *her*. Elizabeth pretended not to understand her, because she knew very well that a serious argument would result from any reply. Mr Collins might never make the offer, and until he did, it was useless to quarrel about him.

If there had not been a ball to get ready for and to talk about, the younger Misses Bennet would have been in a sad state at this time. From the day of the invitation to the day of the ball, continuous rain prevented them from walking to Meryton. No aunt, no officers, no news could be looked for. Even Elizabeth might have found some test of her patience in weather that delayed the development of her acquaintance with Mr Wickham, and nothing less than a dance on Tuesday could have made such a Friday, Saturday, Sunday and Monday bearable to Kitty and Lydia.

♦

On the Tuesday evening, Elizabeth entered the sitting room at Netherfield, and looked without success for Mr Wickham among the group of officers present there. Until then, no doubt about him coming had entered her mind. She had dressed with more care than usual, and readied herself in the highest spirits to complete the winning of his heart. But in a moment the terrible thought came to her that he had been purposely left out of the Bingleys' invitation to the officers, for Mr Darcy's pleasure, and although this was not exactly the case, his friend Mr Denny told them that Wickham had had to go to London on business, and added:

'I do not imagine that he would have gone just now, if he had not wished to avoid a certain gentleman here.'

This information sharpened Elizabeth's feelings of displeasure against Mr Darcy, and although she tried to be cheerful, the first two dances brought a return of unhappiness. Mr Collins, serious and awkward, apologizing instead of paying attention, and often moving wrongly without being conscious of it, brought her all the shame and unhappiness which a disagreeable partner can give.

She danced next with an officer. Then she found herself suddenly addressed by Mr Darcy, who took her so much by surprise in his request for her hand that, without knowing what she did, she accepted him.

Elizabeth took her place in the set, astonished at the honour at which she had arrived in being allowed to stand opposite to Mr Darcy, and seeing in the faces of her neighbours their equal astonishment. They spoke very little until they had finished the dance, when he asked her if she and her sisters did not often walk to Meryton. She answered that this was so, and, unable to stop herself, added, 'When we met you the other day there, we had just been forming a new acquaintance.'

The effect was immediate. The expression on his face became prouder than ever. At last he spoke:

'Mr Wickham is fortunate enough to have such pleasing manners that he can always be sure of *making* friends. It is less certain that he is able to *keep* them.'

'He has been unlucky enough to lose *your* friendship,' replied Elizabeth.

Darcy made no answer, and seemed anxious to change the subject. At that moment Sir William Lucas appeared, and stopped to offer him a mark of attention.

'My dear sir, such very high-class dancing is not often seen. I must hope to have this pleasure often repeated, especially after a certain desirable event,' and he looked towards Jane and Mr Bingley. 'What congratulations will then flow in!'

Sir William's mention of his friend seemed to strike Darcy with some force, and his eyes were directed with a very serious expression towards Bingley and Jane, who were dancing together.

When the dance was over, Miss Bingley came towards Elizabeth, and, with a look of scorn, addressed her as follows:

'So, Miss Eliza, I hear you are quite pleased with George Wickham. But let me warn you not to trust what he says. The story that Mr Darcy has wronged him is completely untrue. He has always been kind to him, though Wickham treated him in a shameful manner. I do not know the details, but I do know that Mr Darcy is not to blame. I pity you, Miss Eliza, but really, considering his family, one could not expect much better.'

'His guilt and his family appear, by your account, to be the same,' said Elizabeth angrily.

'I beg your pardon,' replied Miss Bingley, turning away. 'My words were kindly meant.'

Elizabeth then went in search of her oldest sister, who met her with a smile of such sweet satisfaction that Elizabeth immediately understood her feelings and forgot everything else for the moment in the hope that Jane was on the way to happiness. Jane began to talk about Mr Wickham. 'Mr Bingley does not know the whole of the history, but is sure that his friend has acted rightly and honourably. I am sorry to say that by his account Mr Wickham is not at all a respectable young man.'

'Mr Bingley does not know Mr Wickham himself?'

'No. He never saw him until the other morning at Meryton.'

'This explanation, then, is what he has received from Mr Darcy. I am perfectly satisfied. Mr Bingley has defended his friend, but I shall continue to hold the same opinion.'

She then changed the subject to one more pleasing to them both, and listened with pleasure to the happy hopes which Jane had of Mr Bingley's feelings towards her. When Mr Bingley himself joined them, Elizabeth moved away to Miss Lucas.

Shortly afterwards, Mr Collins came up to them in a state of great excitement. He had discovered that Mr Darcy was a relative of Lady Catherine.

'You are not going to introduce yourself to Mr Darcy?'

'Of course I am.'

Elizabeth tried hard to persuade him against this, warning him that Mr Darcy would consider it as a piece of impoliteness rather than as a mark of respect for his aunt.

'Pardon me for neglecting to take advantage of your advice,' was his reply, 'but in the case before us I consider myself more fitted by education and study to decide on what is right than a young lady like yourself.' And, with that, he left her to approach Mr Darcy, whose astonishment was plain, and who replied with cold politeness.

Elizabeth felt ashamed of her cousin, and turned her attention to the more pleasing subject of Jane's future. Her mother's thoughts were plainly of the same kind, and when they sat down to supper, Elizabeth was deeply annoyed to find that Mrs Bennet was talking loudly to Lady Lucas of nothing else but her expectations that Jane would soon be married to Mr Bingley. Elizabeth tried without success to control her mother's words, because she could see that they were heard by Mr Darcy, who sat opposite them. Nothing she could say had any effect. Elizabeth reddened with shame.

When supper was over, singing was mentioned, and Elizabeth had the added discomfort of seeing Mary getting ready to entertain the company. Mary was the least pretty of the five sisters, so she had tried to make herself more attractive by becoming more able than the others, and was always eager to bring her musical skill to notice. But her powers were by no means fitted for this kind of performance. Her voice was weak, and her manner unnatural. Elizabeth listened with impatience. Mary sang twice, and Elizabeth could see Mr Bingley's sisters exchanging scornful smiles. She looked at her father, who understood and gently stopped his daughter.

The rest of the evening brought Elizabeth little amusement. Mr Collins continued at her side and would not leave her alone. Mr Darcy took no more notice of her, even when he was standing near her.

But Mrs Bennet left Netherfield perfectly satisfied. She was fully confident that she would see Jane married in the course of three or four months. She thought with equal certainty of having another daughter married to Mr Collins. She loved Elizabeth less than her other daughters, and she thought Mr Collins quite good enough for her.

Chapter 7
Mr Collins Makes a Proposal of Marriage

The next day opened a new scene at Longbourn: Mr Collins made a formal proposal of marriage. Having decided to do it without delay, and having no lack of self-confidence, he began in a very orderly manner with all the ceremony which he supposed to be a regular part of the business. On finding Mrs Bennet, Elizabeth and one of the younger girls together soon after breakfast, he addressed the mother in these words:

'May I hope, madam, to speak privately with your lovely daughter Elizabeth?'

Before Elizabeth had time to express her surprise, Mrs Bennet immediately answered:

'Oh, yes, certainly. I am sure that Lizzy can have no objection. Come, Kitty, I want you upstairs.' And picking up her sewing, she was hurrying away, when Elizabeth called out:

'I beg you not to go. Mr Collins must excuse me. He can have nothing to say to me that anybody need not hear. I am going away myself.'

'No, no, nonsense, Lizzy. I desire you to stay where you are.' And when Elizabeth seemed about to escape, she added, 'Lizzy, you must stay and hear Mr Collins.'

Elizabeth could not oppose such a command, and a moment's consideration made her realize that it would be better to get the matter settled, so she sat down again. Mrs Bennet and Kitty walked off, and as soon as they were gone, Mr Collins began:

'Believe me, my dear Miss Elizabeth, your behaviour only adds to your other perfections. You would have been less pleasing in my eyes if there had *not* been this little unwillingness, but allow me to inform you that I have your respected mother's permission for this address. Almost as soon as I entered this house, I made you my choice as the companion of my future life. My reasons for marrying are, first, I think it a right thing for every church minister to set an example by doing so; secondly, I am sure that it will add very greatly to my happiness; and thirdly, Lady Catherine has advised it. As I am heir to this property on the death of your honoured father, I decided to choose my wife from among his daughters. I know very well that you have little fortune, but I shall never blame you for that when we are married.'

It was necessary to stop him now.

'You are in too much of a hurry, sir,' she cried. 'You forget that I have made no answer. Accept my thanks for the honour that you are showing me, but it is impossible for me to do otherwise than to refuse your proposal.'

'I quite understand,' replied Mr Collins, with a wave of the hand, 'that it is usual for young ladies to refuse the man whom they secretly mean to accept, when he asks for the first time.'

'On my honour, sir,' cried Elizabeth, 'I am perfectly serious in my refusal.'

'When I next speak to you on this subject,' continued Mr Collins, 'I shall expect to receive a more favourable answer.'

Elizabeth tried without success to make him believe her. He had too good an opinion of himself and his position, and he pointed out that she was too poor to receive many other offers. To this she could make no reply, and immediately, and in silence, left the room, with the intention of asking for her father's support.

♦

Mrs Bennet had waited in the hall for the end of the conversation. As soon as she saw Elizabeth open the door and, with a quick step, pass her towards the stairway, she entered the breakfast room and congratulated both Mr Collins and herself. Mr Collins received and returned these good wishes, but when he went on to give details of his conversation with Elizabeth, the information astonished Mrs Bennet.

'But you may depend on it, Mr Collins,' she added, 'that Lizzy shall be made to behave reasonably. I will speak to her myself immediately. She is a very foolish girl, and does not know her own interest, but I will *make* her know it. I will go to Mr Bennet, and we shall very soon settle the matter with her, I am sure.'

She would not give him time to reply, but hurried immediately to her husband, and called out as she entered the library: 'Oh, Mr Bennet, you are wanted immediately. You must come and make Lizzy marry Mr Collins, because she swears she will not have him.'

Mr Bennet raised his eyes from his book as she entered, and fixed them on her face with a calm unconcern which was not in the least changed by her information.

'I have not the pleasure of understanding you,' he said, when she had finished her speech. 'What are you talking about?'

'Mr Collins and Lizzy. Lizzy says that she will not have Mr Collins, and if you do not hurry, he will change his mind and not have *her*.'

'And what am I to do about it? It seems a hopeless business.'

'Speak to Lizzy about it yourself. Tell her that she must marry him.'

'Let her be called down. She shall hear my opinion.'

Mrs Bennet rang the bell and Miss Elizabeth was sent for.

'Come here, child,' said her father as she appeared. 'I have sent for you on an affair of importance. I understand that Mr Collins has made you an offer of marriage. Is it true?' Elizabeth replied that it was. 'Very well – and you have refused this offer of marriage?'

'I have, sir.'

'Very well. We now come to the point. Your mother demands

that you accept it. Is it not so, Mrs Bennet?'

'Yes, or I will never see her again.'

'An unhappy choice is before you, Elizabeth. From this day you will be a stranger to one of your parents. Your mother will never see you again if you do *not* marry Mr Collins, and I will never see you again if you *do*.'

Elizabeth could not help smiling at such an ending to such a beginning. Mrs Bennet, on the other hand, was extremely disappointed. She returned to the subject repeatedly, using both persuasion and threats to try and change her daughter's mind. Mr Collins himself remained silent and offended, unable to understand how his cousin could possibly refuse him.

While the family were in this state, Charlotte Lucas came to spend the day with them. Mr Collins's attentions were now turned to her, which Elizabeth found to be a great relief.

Chapter 8   Netherfield Is Empty

After breakfast the next day, the girls walked to Meryton to inquire if Mr Wickham had returned. He joined them as they entered the town, and went with them to their aunt's. He explained to Elizabeth his absence from the ball.

'I found,' he said, 'as the time approached, that I had better not meet Mr Darcy – that to be in his company might be more than I could bear.'

Elizabeth highly approved of his good sense. As Wickham and another officer walked back with them to Longbourn, she was able to introduce him to her father and mother.

Soon after their return, a letter was delivered to Miss Bennet. It came from Netherfield, and was opened immediately. Elizabeth saw her sister's face change as she read it. But she soon controlled herself and, putting the letter away, tried to join in the conversation with her usual cheerfulness. But as soon as the officers had left, a look from Jane invited Elizabeth to follow her upstairs.

When they had reached their own room, Jane, taking out the letter, said, 'This is from Caroline Bingley. What it contains has surprised me a great deal. The whole party have left Netherfield by this time, and are on their way to town, and without any intention of coming back again.'

She then read the letter out loud. It spoke of the writer's sorrow at parting from Jane, and urged her to write frequently. Elizabeth judged this to be insincere. It stated that Mr Bingley had business in town, and would be in no hurry to leave it again.

'It is clear from this that he will come back no more this winter,' said Jane.

'It is clear that Miss Bingley does not intend that he *should*.'

'Why do you think so? It must be his own decision. He is free to act as he wishes. But you do not know everything. I will read you the words that hurt me most. I will have no secrets from you.' The letter then told of the beauty of Mr Darcy's young sister, and of Mr Bingley's admiration for her, and of the family's hopes that they would marry.

'Is it not clear enough? Does it not plainly state that Caroline neither expects nor wishes me to be her sister, and that she believes that her brother does not care for me? She means – most kindly – to warn me. Can there be any other opinion on the subject?'

'Yes, there can. Mine is totally different. Miss Bingley sees that her brother is in love with you, and wants him to marry Miss Darcy. She follows him to town in the hope of keeping him there, and tries to persuade you that he does not care about you.'

Jane shook her head.

'Really, Jane, you ought to believe me. No one who has ever seen you together can doubt his love. But the case is this – we are

37

not rich enough or grand enough for them.'

Elizabeth spoke comfortingly to her sister, and gradually persuaded her that Mr Bingley would return later and answer every wish of her heart. To their mother they decided only to announce that the Netherfield party had left for a short time.

Chapter 9   Mr Collins Makes Another Proposal

The Bennets were invited to dinner with the Lucases, and again, most of the time, Miss Lucas was kind enough to listen to Mr Collins. Elizabeth thanked her warmly, and Charlotte told her friend that she was glad to be of service to her. This was very helpful of her, but the real reason for Charlotte's kindness was something that Elizabeth had no idea of – a desire to attract Mr Collins herself. When they parted later that night, Charlotte would have felt almost certain of success if he had not been planning to leave Longbourn. But Mr Collins, wasting no time, escaped from the Bennets early next morning with great skill. Miss Lucas noticed him from an upper window as he walked towards her parents' house. She came down quickly to the garden, and there, meeting him as if by accident, received his proposal of marriage.

Sir William and Lady Lucas were immediately asked for their agreement, which they willingly gave. Mr Collins's present position made it a good marriage for their daughter, to whom they could give little fortune, and in the future he would be Mr Bennet's heir. Charlotte was fairly well satisfied. Mr Collins was neither sensible nor agreeable, but she, on the other hand, was twenty-seven, and with little chance of other offers.

She decided to give the news to the Bennets herself, and therefore asked Mr Collins to say nothing when he returned to Longbourn, which he was leaving the next day.

When Elizabeth was privately informed by Charlotte, her astonishment was so great that she could not help crying out:

'Engaged to be married to Mr Collins! My dear Charlotte, impossible!'

'I see what you are feeling,' replied Charlotte. 'You must be surprised, very much surprised, as Mr Collins was so recently wanting to marry you. But I do not expect very much from marriage, you know. I shall be satisfied with having a comfortable home.'

Elizabeth answered quietly and, after an awkward pause, they returned to the rest of the family. Charlotte did not stay much longer, and Elizabeth was left to think over what she had heard. The strangeness of Mr Collins's making two offers of marriage within three days was nothing in comparison with his being now accepted. She would never have expected Charlotte to give up her finer feelings to gain no more than comfort. She felt that her friend had shamed herself, and she did not believe it possible for her to be happy in the life she had chosen.

As for Mrs Bennet, she was astonished and shocked by the news. A week passed before she could see Elizabeth without scolding her, and a month before she could speak to Sir William or Lady Lucas without being rude. Lady Lucas was not without pleasure in being able to talk to Mrs Bennet about the comfort of having a daughter well married, and she visited Longbourn rather oftener than usual, to say how happy she was. Between Elizabeth and Charlotte there was an awkwardness that kept them silent on the subject. Elizabeth felt that there could never be any real confidence between them again, and she turned with greater fondness to her sister Jane, for whose happiness she became daily more anxious.

Chapter 10   Jane Goes to London

Neither Jane nor Elizabeth was comfortable on the subject of Mr Bingley's continued absence. Even Elizabeth began to fear, not that Bingley's feelings had changed, but that his sisters and the amusements of London would be successful in keeping him away. Jane wished to hide her anxiety, and never mentioned it, but an hour rarely passed without some remark from her mother which it needed all Jane's patience to bear in silence.

Mrs Bennet was really in a most pitiable state. She was continually thinking about why Mr Bingley had not returned. Then, too, the sight of Miss Lucas was hateful to her. She regarded her with jealous dislike as the wife of the future owner of Longbourn. Whenever Charlotte came to see them, Mrs Bennet imagined that she was thinking of the time when she would take possession.

Jane had written to Miss Bingley, and in a little while a reply arrived and put an end to doubt. The first sentence announced that they were all settled in London for the winter, and the letter ended with her brother's sadness at not having had time to say goodbye to his friends before leaving.

Hope was over, completely over. Elizabeth's heart was divided between sympathy for her sister and anger against the others. Secretly she blamed Mr Bingley for his weakness in being persuaded by his sisters, and she was angry because she believed that Mr Darcy had helped to influence him.

Jane bore her sorrow with gentle sweetness, and tried to believe that she had only imagined Mr Bingley to be fond of her, and that she had only herself to blame.

◆

On the following Monday, Mrs Bennet had the pleasure of receiving her brother and his wife, who came, as usual, from

London to spend Christmas at Longbourn. Mr Gardiner was a sensible, gentlemanly man, of much finer character than his sister, and Mrs Gardiner, who was several years younger than Mrs Bennet, was a pleasant, intelligent, well-dressed woman, and a great favourite with her nieces.

The first part of Mrs Gardiner's business, on her arrival, was to give her presents and describe the newest fashions. When this was done, she had a less active part to play. It became her turn to listen. Mrs Bennet had many troubles to tell, and much to complain of. Two of her girls had been on the point of marriage, but nothing had happened after all.

'I do not blame Jane,' she continued, 'but Lizzy! Oh, sister! It is very hard to think that she might have been Mr Collins's wife by this time, if it had not been for her own bad character! He made her an offer, here in this room, and she refused him. The result of all this is that Lady Lucas will have a daughter married before I have. It is very bad for my nerves to be annoyed so by my own family. But your coming at this time is the greatest of comforts, and I am glad to hear about the new dresses.'

When Mrs Gardiner was alone with Elizabeth afterwards, she spoke on the subject of Jane.

'Poor Jane! I am sorry for her, because, with her character, she may not recover for some time from such a disappointment. But do you think that she could be persuaded to go back to town with us? A change of scene might be of help to her.'

Elizabeth was extremely pleased with this proposal.

'I hope,' added Mrs Gardiner, 'that no thought of this young man will influence her. We live in such a different part of the town, and mix with such a different class of society, that she is not likely to meet him, unless he really comes to see her.'

Miss Bennet accepted her aunt's invitation with pleasure, and the Gardiners left Longbourn after a week's stay. Before she went, though, Mrs Gardiner, who guessed from Elizabeth's behaviour her feelings for Wickham, gave her a word of advice.

'Seriously, I would advise you to be careful. I have nothing to say against *him*. He is a most interesting young man, and if he had the fortune that he ought to have, I should think that you could not do better. But as it is – you have sense, and we all expect you to use it. You must not disappoint your father.'

♦

January and February were dull months. Elizabeth missed Jane sadly. Charlotte was married and had left for Hunsford. There was little except the walks to Meryton, sometimes muddy and sometimes cold, to help pass the time.

Elizabeth wrote and received many letters. She exchanged news with Charlotte as regularly as ever, but their friendship could never be as close as it had been before. From London Jane wrote that she had neither seen nor heard anything of Miss Bingley. But she accounted for this by supposing that her last letter to her friend had by some accident been lost.

'My aunt,' she continued, 'is going tomorrow into that part of the town, and I shall take the opportunity of visiting Caroline.'

She wrote again after she had made the visit. 'I did not think that Caroline was in good spirits,' were her words, 'but she was glad to see me and cross that I had given her no notice of my coming to London. I was right, therefore. My last letter had never reached her. I inquired after her brother, of course. He is so busy in society that they hardly ever see him. My visit was not long, as Caroline and Mrs Hurst were going out.'

Elizabeth shook her head over this letter.

Four weeks passed, and Jane saw nothing of Mr Bingley. She could no longer be blind to Miss Bingley's inattention. At last the visitor did appear, but the shortness of her stay and the change in her manner no longer made it possible for Jane to deceive herself. It was plain that she received no pleasure from coming. She made a slight, formal apology for not visiting her before, said not a word about wishing to see her again, and was in every way so unfriendly that Jane decided not to continue the acquaintance.

To Mrs Gardiner, Elizabeth wrote of her own affairs. Wickham's attentions to her were over, and he was now the admirer of Miss Mary King, a young lady whose grandfather had just died and left her ten thousand pounds. Elizabeth's heart had been only slightly touched, and her pride was satisfied with believing that *she* would have been his only choice, if fortune had permitted.

Chapter 11   Elizabeth Visits Hunsford

In March, Elizabeth was visiting Hunsford, at Charlotte's invitation. She had not at first thought very seriously of going there, but she found that her friend was depending on the arrangement. Absence had increased her desire to see Charlotte again, and lessened her disgust for Mr Collins. The journey would also give her a moment with Jane as she would spend the night in London. She would travel with Sir William Lucas and his second daughter Maria.

It was only 24 miles to London, and they began early so that they could arrive before midday. As they drove to Mr Gardiner's door, Jane was at a sitting room window watching for their arrival. When they entered the hall, she was there to welcome them, and Elizabeth, looking closely at her face, was pleased to see it as healthy and beautiful as ever. On the stairs was a crowd of little girls and boys, whose eagerness for their cousin's appearance would not allow them to wait in the sitting room, and whose shyness, as they had not seen her for a year, prevented them from coming down any further.

All was joy and kindness. The day passed away most pleasantly, the afternoon in shopping, and the evening at one of the theatres.

During the performance, Elizabeth managed to sit by her aunt. Their first subject was her sister, and she was more troubled than surprised to hear that, though Jane struggled to be cheerful, there were times when she was very sad. It was reasonable, though, to hope that this would not continue for too long.

Before they were separated by the end of the play, Elizabeth had the unexpected happiness of an invitation to go with her uncle and aunt on a tour which they planned to take in the summer.

'We have not quite decided how far it will take us,' said Mrs Gardiner, 'but perhaps to the Lakes.'

No plan could have been more welcome to Elizabeth, and her acceptance of the invitation was immediate and grateful.

♦

Every object in the next day's journey was new and interesting to Elizabeth. When they left the main road for the smaller road to Hunsford, every eye was in search of the Parsonage. At last it appeared. Mr Collins and Charlotte were at the door, and the carriage stopped at the small gate among the smiles and greetings of the whole party. Mrs Collins welcomed her friend with the greatest pleasure, and Elizabeth was more and more pleased that she had come, as she found herself so warmly received.

She could not help thinking, as Mr Collins proudly showed her his house and furniture, that he wished to make her feel what she had lost by refusing him. She was not able to please him, though, by any sign of unhappiness; instead she looked with surprise at her friend, who could appear so cheerful with such a companion. After admiring the house, they were invited by their host to take a walk in the garden. One of his chief pleasures was to work in the garden, and Elizabeth smiled to herself as she heard Charlotte talk of the healthiness of the exercise, and say that she encouraged it as much as possible.

The house itself, though small, was neat and convenient, and when Mr Collins could be forgotten, there was a great feeling of comfort everywhere – and by Charlotte's enjoyment, which was quite plain, Elizabeth supposed he must often be forgotten.

It was mentioned at dinner that Lady Catherine was still in the country. Mr Collins poured out his praises of her kind attentions to himself and Charlotte, and expressed the expectation that she would honour Elizabeth with her notice.

The evening was spent chiefly in talking over the news from home, and when it had passed, Elizabeth, in the quietness of her own room, had to think over Charlotte's degree of satisfaction, to understand her skill in guiding her husband, and her self-control in managing to deal with him, and to admit that it was well done.

At around the middle of the next day, as she was in her room getting ready for a walk, a sudden noise below showed the whole house to be in a state of excitement, and, after listening for a moment, Elizabeth heard somebody running upstairs in a violent hurry, and calling loudly to her. She opened the door, and met Maria, who cried to her to come down that moment.

Elizabeth asked questions without success. Maria would tell her nothing more, and they ran down to the dining room in search of the cause of her excitement. It was two ladies stopping in a carriage at the garden gate.

'And is this all?' cried Elizabeth. 'I expected at least that the pigs had got into the garden, and here is nothing but Lady Catherine and her daughter!'

'My dear!' said Maria, quite shocked at the mistake. 'It is not Lady Catherine. The old lady is Mrs Jenkinson, who lives with them. The other is Miss de Bourgh. Only look at her. Who would have thought she could be so thin and small!'

'I like her appearance,' said Elizabeth, who was struck with other ideas. 'She looks weak and disagreeable. Yes, she will suit him very well. She will make him a very fitting wife.'

Chapter 12   Lady Catherine de Bourgh

The purpose of the ladies' visit had been to ask the whole party to dinner at Rosings, where Lady Catherine lived, and Mr Collins's proud excitement at this invitation was complete. Hardly anything else was talked of the whole day. Mr Collins carefully explained what they should expect, so that the sight of such rooms, so many servants, and so excellent a dinner would not completely astonish them. While they were dressing, he came two or three times to their doors to urge them to be quick, as Lady Catherine very much objected to being kept waiting for dinner. Such accounts quite frightened Maria Lucas, who had been little used to society, but Elizabeth's courage did not fail her. She had heard nothing of Lady Catherine that filled her with respect for cleverness or goodness, and she thought that she could meet the grandness of money and rank without fear.

Elizabeth found herself quite equal to the occasion when she was introduced to Lady Catherine, and was able to look at the three ladies in front of her calmly. Lady Catherine was a tall, large woman, with strongly marked features. Her behaviour was not friendly, and her manner of receiving them did not allow her visitors to forget their inferior rank. Whatever she said was spoken in a commanding voice that expressed her belief in her own importance. Miss de Bourgh looked pale and weak, and spoke only in a low voice to Mrs Jenkinson.

The dinner was extremely fine, and all was as Mr Collins had promised. His loud praises of everything were continually repeated by Sir William. Lady Catherine smiled at them, and seemed pleased by their extreme admiration.

When the ladies returned to the sitting room, there was little to be done except listen to Lady Catherine talk, which she did without stopping, giving her opinion loudly on every subject in a manner that showed that she was not used to having her judgment opposed. She asked Elizabeth many things about her family: their number, their education, whether any of them was likely to be married, and what her mother's name had been before marriage. Elizabeth felt all the impoliteness of these questions, but answered them calmly. Lady Catherine then asked:

'Do you play and sing, Miss Bennet?'

'A little.'

'Oh, then – some time or other we shall be happy to hear you. Our piano is a very good one – probably much better than – do your sisters play and sing?'

'One of them does.'

'Why did you not all learn? You ought all to have learned. Do you draw?'

'No, not at all.'

'What, none of you?'

'Not one.'

'That is very strange. But I suppose you had no opportunity. Are any of your younger sisters out in society,★ Miss Bennet?'

'Yes, all of them.'

'All! What, all five at the same time? Very strange! And you only the second. What is your age?'

'With three younger sisters grown up,' replied Elizabeth smiling, 'you can hardly expect me to speak on that subject.'

Lady Catherine seemed quite astonished at not receiving a direct answer, and Elizabeth thought that perhaps she was the first person who had dared to speak to her in that way.

★out in society: considered old enough to attend dinner parties, balls and other social events.

47

'You cannot be more than twenty, I am sure – therefore you need not hide your age.'

'I am not yet twenty-one.'

When the gentlemen joined them, the card tables were placed. At one table Lady Catherine played with Sir William and with Mr and Mrs Collins; at the other, Miss de Bourgh with Mrs Jenkinson and the two girls. Lady Catherine continued to talk, pointing out the mistakes made by others. Mr Collins agreed with everything she said, thanking her for every game he won, and apologizing if he thought he had won too many. Hardly a word was spoken at the other table, and Elizabeth found the game extremely boring.

Chapter 13   Visitors to Rosings

In a quiet way, with walks and occasional visits to Rosings, the first two weeks of Elizabeth's stay soon passed. Sir William Lucas had returned home, but the next week brought an addition to the family at Rosings. Mr Darcy was expected, and when he came, he brought with him Colonel Fitzwilliam, his cousin.

The day after their arrival, they came to the Parsonage. Colonel Fitzwilliam was about thirty, not very good-looking, but in person and manners most truly a gentleman. Mr Darcy looked just as he had always done, was polite but spoke little. Elizabeth only lowered her head in greeting without saying a word.

Colonel Fitzwilliam entered into conversation directly, with the confidence of a man of good family. After a long silence, Mr Darcy inquired after the health of Elizabeth's family. She answered him in the usual way and, after a moment's pause, added: 'My oldest sister has been in town during the last three months. Have you not seen her?'

She thought that he looked a little confused as he answered

that he had not been so fortunate as to meet Miss Bennet.

It was some days before the next invitation came from Rosings. While there were visitors in the house, the company from the Parsonage were not necessary. When the invitation did arrive, and they joined the party in Lady Catherine's sitting room, Lady Catherine received them politely, but it was clear that they were not as welcome as they had been when she could get nobody else.

Colonel Fitzwilliam seemed really glad to see them. Anything was a welcome relief at Rosings, and Mrs Collins's pretty friend had attracted him. He now seated himself by her, and talked so agreeably that Elizabeth had never been half so well entertained in that room before. Their conversation was so full of spirit that it drew the attention of Lady Catherine herself. As for Mr Darcy, his eyes had been soon and repeatedly turned towards them with a look of interest. At last Lady Catherine called out:

'What are you saying, Fitzwilliam? What is it you are talking of? What are you telling Miss Bennet?'

'We are speaking of music, madam,' he said.

'Of music! Then please speak out loud. I must have my share in the conversation, if you are speaking of music. There are few people in England, I suppose, who have a better natural taste in music than myself. I would have been an excellent performer.'

She then inquired after the playing of Darcy's sister, Georgiana, and he spoke in brotherly praise of her skill.

'She must practise continually,' Lady Catherine went on. 'I have told Miss Bennet several times that she will never play really well unless she practises more, and though Mrs Collins has no instrument, she is very welcome to come to Rosings every day and play the piano in Mrs Jenkinson's room. She would be in nobody's way, you know, in that part of the house.'

Mr Darcy looked a little ashamed of his aunt's lack of good manners, and said nothing.

When coffee was over, Colonel Fitzwilliam reminded Elizabeth that she had promised to play to him, and she sat down immediately at the piano. He pulled a chair up near her. Lady Catherine listened to half a song and then talked to her other nephew, until Darcy walked away from her, and, moving towards the piano, positioned himself so that he had a view of the performer's face. Elizabeth saw what he was doing, and at the first convenient pause turned to him with a smile and said:

'You mean to frighten me, Mr Darcy, by coming with all this ceremony to hear me. But I will not be afraid, though your sister *does* play so well.'

'I shall not say that you are mistaken,' he replied, 'because you could not really suppose me to have any intention of frightening you.'

Elizabeth laughed, and said to Colonel Fitzwilliam: 'Your cousin will teach you not to believe a word I say. It makes me want to behave badly towards him.'

'Then let me hear why you are angry with him,' said Colonel Fitzwilliam.

'You shall hear – but be ready for something very terrible. The first time I ever saw him was at a ball – and what do you think he did at this ball? He danced only four dances, though there were very few gentlemen and, to my certain knowledge, more than one young lady was sitting down for lack of a partner.'

'I had not at that time the honour of knowing any lady there, except from my own party.'

'True, but can nobody ever be introduced in a ballroom?'

'Perhaps,' said Darcy, 'I would have behaved better if I had asked for an introduction, but I am not someone who can easily make friends with strangers.'

'Shall we ask your cousin the reason for this?' said Elizabeth, addressing Colonel Fitzwilliam.

'I can answer your question,' said Fitzwilliam. 'It is because he will not give himself the trouble.'

'I have certainly not the ability that some people possess,' said Darcy, 'of holding a conversation easily with those whom I have never seen before.'

Here they were interrupted by Lady Catherine, who called out to know what they were talking about. Elizabeth immediately began to play again. Lady Catherine came nearer, and, after listening for a few minutes, said to Darcy:

'She uses her fingers well, though her taste is not equal to Anne's. Anne would have been a truly great performer if her health had allowed her to learn.'

Elizabeth looked at Darcy to see whether he agreed with this praise of his cousin, but neither at that moment nor at any other could she see any sign of love. Lady Catherine continued her remarks on Elizabeth's performance until her carriage was ready to take them all home.

◆

Elizabeth was sitting by herself the next morning writing to Jane, while Mrs Collins and Maria were gone on business into the village, when she was interrupted by a ring at the front door, the signal of a visitor. When the door of the room was opened, to her great surprise Mr Darcy, and Mr Darcy alone, entered.

He seemed astonished, too, to find her alone, and apologized for the interruption by letting her know that he had expected all the ladies to be at home.

They then sat down, and when her inquiries after Rosings were made, seemed in danger of sinking into total silence. It was necessary, therefore, to speak of something, so, wanting to know what he would say on the subject of their leaving Netherfield so quickly, she remarked:

'How very suddenly you all left Netherfield last November,

Mr Darcy! Mr Bingley and his sisters were well, I hope, when you left London?'

'Perfectly so, thank you.'

After a short pause, she added:

'I understand that Mr Bingley has not much idea of ever returning to Netherfield again?'

'It is probable that he may spend very little of his time there in future.'

'If he means to be very little at Netherfield, it would be better for the neighbourhood that he should give up the place completely, for then we might possibly get a settled family there.'

'I should not be surprised,' said Darcy, 'if he were to give it up, if he found another property that suited him.'

Elizabeth made no answer. She was afraid of talking longer of his friend, and, having nothing else to say, was now determined to leave the trouble of finding a subject to him.

He understood, and very soon began with, 'Mr Collins appears to be very fortunate in his choice of a wife. It must be very pleasant for her to be settled within such an easy distance of her own family and friends.'

'An easy distance, do you call it? It is nearly 50 miles. I should never have said that Mrs Collins was settled near her family.'

'It is a proof of your own close ties to your home. Anything beyond the very neighbourhood of Longbourn, I suppose, would appear far.'

Then he moved his chair a little towards her, and said, '*You* cannot have a right to such very strong local feeling. *You* cannot always have been at Longbourn.'

Elizabeth looked surprised. The gentleman experienced some change of feeling. He moved his chair back again, took a newspaper from the table, and said in a colder voice:

'Are you pleased with Kent?'

A short conversation on the subject of the country followed. It was soon brought to an end by the entrance of Charlotte and her sister, who had just returned from their walk.

'What can be the meaning of this?' said Charlotte, as soon as Darcy was gone. 'My dear Eliza, he must be in love with you, or he would never have visited us in this familiar way.'

But when Elizabeth told of his silence, it did not seem very likely to be the case, and they could only suppose his visit to result from the difficulty of finding anything to do at that time of year. Gentlemen cannot always stay indoors, and the nearness of the Parsonage encouraged the two cousins, from this period, to walk there almost every day, sometimes separately and sometimes together. It was plain that Colonel Fitzwilliam came because he found pleasure in their society, but Mr Darcy could not come for that reason, because he frequently sat there for ten minutes at a time without opening his lips. Mrs Collins did not know how to explain it. He certainly looked at Elizabeth a great deal, and she once or twice suggested to her friend the possibility that he was interested in her, but Elizabeth always laughed at the idea.

Chapter 14   Mr Darcy

During Elizabeth's daily walk within the park of Rosings, which the people at the Parsonage were permitted to visit, she more than once unexpectedly met Mr Darcy. To prevent it ever happening again, she took care on the first occasion to inform him that it was her favourite part. It was very strange, therefore, that it happened a second time. But it did, and even a third. He actually thought it necessary to turn back and walk with her. He never said a great deal, and she did not give herself the trouble of talking or listening much.

One day she was reading Jane's last letter again as she walked, when, instead of being again surprised by Mr Darcy, she looked up and saw that Colonel Fitzwilliam was coming to meet her. They walked together towards the Parsonage.

'Is it settled that you leave Kent on Saturday?' she asked.

'Yes – if Darcy does not put it off again. But he arranges our business just as he pleases. I share with him the responsibility of looking after Miss Darcy.'

'Do you really? And does she give you much trouble? Young ladies of her age are sometimes difficult to manage.'

As she spoke, she saw him looking at her very seriously, and his manner made her believe that she had somehow or other got fairly near the truth. She replied immediately:

'You need not be frightened. I have never heard any harm of her. She is a great favourite of some ladies of my acquaintance, Mrs Hurst and Miss Bingley. I think that you know them.'

'I know them a little. Their brother is a great friend of Darcy's.'

'Oh, yes,' said Elizabeth sharply, 'Mr Darcy is uncommonly kind to Mr Bingley, and takes great care of him.'

'Care of him! Yes, I really believe Darcy *does* take care of him. From something that he told me, I have reason to think that Bingley must have cause to be very grateful to him.'

'What do you mean?'

'It is a matter which Darcy, of course, could not wish to be generally known, because if it were to reach the lady's family it would be an unpleasant thing.'

'You may depend on my not mentioning it.'

'What he told me was this: that he congratulated himself on having saved a friend from the inconveniences of a most unwise marriage, but without mentioning names or any other details.'

'Did Mr Darcy give you his reasons for his involvement?'

'I understood that there were some very strong objections to the lady.'

Elizabeth walked on, her heart swelling with anger. She could not trust herself further with the subject, and therefore, quickly changing the conversation, talked about different matters until they reached the Parsonage. There, shut in her own room as soon as their visitor had left them, she could think without interruption of all that she had heard. She had never doubted that Mr Darcy had been involved in the action taken to separate Mr Bingley and Jane, but she had always blamed Miss Bingley as the chief person responsible. But now she knew. *He* was the cause – his pride was the cause – of all that Jane had suffered. He had ruined every hope of happiness for the most loving, most generous heart in the world.

'There were some very strong objections to the lady,' were Colonel Fitzwilliam's words, and these strong objections probably included her having one uncle who was a country lawyer and another who was in business in London.

'To Jane herself,' she whispered, 'there could be no possible objection – she is all beauty and goodness! Her understanding is excellent, her mind improved, and her manners excellent. Neither could my father be to blame, since he has abilities that Mr Darcy himself could not fail to respect.' But when she thought of her mother her confidence *did* weaken a little.

The excitement and tears which the subject caused brought on a headache, and it became so much worse towards the evening that, added to her unwillingness to see Mr Darcy, it made her decide not to go with her cousins to Rosings, where they were invited to take tea. Mrs Collins, seeing that she was really unwell, did not urge her to go, and prevented her husband as much as possible from urging her, but Mr Collins could not hide his fear that Lady Catherine might be rather displeased by her staying at home.

◆

When they had gone, Elizabeth, as if intending to sharpen her anger as much as possible against Mr Darcy, chose for her employment the examination of all the letters which Jane had written to her since her arrival in Kent. They contained no actual complaint, but in all, and in almost every line of each, there was a lack of the cheerfulness that had always been natural to her. Mr Darcy's shameful pride in what he had been able to cause gave Elizabeth a keener sense of her sister's sufferings.

At this point she was suddenly interrupted by the sound of the doorbell and, to her complete astonishment, she saw Mr Darcy walk into the room. In a hurried manner he immediately began an inquiry after her health. She answered him with cold politeness. He sat down for a few moments, and then, getting up, walked around the room. Elizabeth was surprised, but did not say a word. After a silence of several minutes, he came towards her in a troubled manner, and began to speak:

'I have struggled without success. My feelings will not be controlled. You must allow me to tell you how warmly I admire and love you.'

Elizabeth's astonishment was beyond expression. She looked away, red in the face, and was silent. He considered this enough encouragement, and the expression of all that he felt for her immediately followed.

He spoke well, but there were other feelings to be described besides those of his heart, and his words were more concerned with pride than love. His sense of her inferiority, his feeling that he was lowering himself, the family considerations that had caused his judgment to oppose his preference, all were expressed with a force that was unlikely to make his proposal acceptable.

In spite of her deeply rooted dislike, she could not fail to realize what an honour it was to receive such a man's attention, and though her intentions did not change for one moment, she was at first sorry for the pain that he would receive, until, insulted by his language as he continued, she lost all pity in anger. She tried to control herself, so she could answer him patiently when he had finished. He ended by expressing the hope that he would now be rewarded by her acceptance of his hand in marriage. As he said this, she could clearly see that he had no doubt of a favourable answer. Such confidence could only increase her annoyance, and when he had ended, the colour in her face deepened and she said:

'If I could feel grateful, as I believe one should in such a situation, I would now thank you. But I cannot – I have never desired your good opinion, and you have certainly given it most unwillingly. The reasons which, you tell me, have long prevented the expression of your feelings, can have little difficulty in bringing them under control.'

Mr Darcy, whose eyes were fixed on her face, seemed to hear her words with no less anger than surprise. He became pale, and the confusion in his mind was plain in every feature. Finally, in a voice of forced calmness, he said:

'And this is all the reply which I am to have the honour of expecting! I might, perhaps, wish to be informed why, with so little attempt at politeness, I am refused.'

'I might as well inquire,' she replied, 'why, with so clear an intention of insulting me, you chose to tell me that you liked me against your will. Was that not some excuse for impoliteness, if I was impolite? But I have other reasons. Do you think that any consideration would lead me to accept the man who has been the means of ruining, perhaps for ever, the happiness of my most dearly loved sister?'

As she spoke these words, Mr Darcy's face changed colour, but he listened without interrupting her while she continued:

'Nothing can excuse the unjust and ungenerous part that you played there. You cannot state that you have not been the chief, if not the only means of dividing the pair of them.'

She paused, and saw that he was listening in a manner that proved him to be unmoved.

'Is it not true that you have done it?' she repeated.

He then replied with calmness: 'Yes, it is true that I did everything in my power to separate my friend from your sister, and that I am glad of my success. I have been kinder towards him than towards myself.'

Elizabeth appeared not to notice this polite remark, but its meaning did not escape her, nor was it likely to soften her feelings.

'But it is not only this affair,' she continued, 'on which my dislike is based. Long before, your character was made plain in the story which I received many months ago from Mr Wickham.'

'You take an eager interest in that gentleman's concerns,' said Darcy, in a more troubled voice, and with deeper colour in his face.

'No one who knows his misfortunes can help feeling an interest in him.'

'His misfortunes!' repeated Darcy scornfully. 'Yes, his misfortunes have been great.'

'And you are responsible,' cried Elizabeth with energy. '*You* have reduced him to his present state.'

'And this,' cried Darcy, as he walked with quick steps across the room, 'is your opinion of me. I thank you for explaining it so fully. But perhaps,' he added, stopping in his walk, and turning towards her, 'these offences might have been forgiven if your pride had not been hurt by my honest explanation of the reasons that made me wait so long. I am not ashamed of the feelings that I expressed. They were natural and fair. Could you expect me to be happy about the inferiority of your relations?'

Elizabeth felt herself becoming more angry every moment, but she tried to speak calmly as she said:

'You could not have made me the offer of your hand in any

possible way that would have led me to accept it.'

Again his astonishment was clear. She went on:

'From the very beginning, your manners struck me as showing the greatest pride in yourself and scorn for the feelings of others, and I had not known you a month before I felt that you were the last man in the world whom I could ever be persuaded to marry.'

'You have said quite enough, madam. Forgive me for having wasted so much of your time, and accept my best wishes for your health and happiness.'

And with these words he quickly left the room.

The disorder of Elizabeth's mind was now painfully great, and from actual weakness she sat down and cried for half an hour. Her astonishment increased every moment. That she should receive an offer of marriage from Mr Darcy! That he should be so much in love with her that he wished to marry her in spite of all the objections that had made him prevent his friend's marrying her sister, and which must appear equally strong in his own case! And his shameful pride! His shameless admission of what he had done with regard to Jane! His unfeeling manner, his cruelty towards Mr Wickham!

She continued with these unhappy thoughts until the sound of the others returning from Rosings made her hurry away to her own room.

Chapter 15   Elizabeth Receives a Letter

Elizabeth woke the next morning to the same thoughts. It was impossible to fix her mind on anything else, so she decided soon after breakfast to give herself air and exercise. She was going directly towards her favourite part of the park, when she remembered that Mr Darcy sometimes came there, and she turned up the narrow road outside Rosings.

After a little time she caught sight of a gentleman within the park. She had turned away, but when she heard a voice calling her, though it was Mr Darcy's, she moved towards the gate. He, too, had reached it by this time. Holding out a letter, he said, with a look of proud calm, 'Will you do me the honour of reading this?' Then he turned and was soon out of sight.

Elizabeth opened the letter and saw two sheets, completely covered in handwriting. The letter had been written at Rosings, at eight o'clock in the morning, and read as follows:

Do not be troubled, madam, on receiving this letter. I write without any intention of upsetting you, or wounding my own self-respect, by mentioning unnecessarily what passed between us last night. But my character demands this to be written and read. You must, therefore, pardon the freedom with which I ask your attention. You will, I know, give it unwillingly, but I must request it as a matter of justice.

Last night, you charged me with two offences of a very different kind. The first was that I had separated Mr Bingley from your sister, and the other that I had ruined the hopes of Mr Wickham. I must now explain these matters.

I had not been in Hertfordshire for long before I saw that Bingley preferred your oldest sister to any other young woman there. I did not take this seriously, because I had often seen him in love before. But at the ball at Netherfield, while I had the honour of dancing with you, I first realized, through Sir William Lucas's accidental information, that Bingley's attentions to your sister had caused a general expectation that they would be married. From that moment I watched my friend carefully, and saw that his attraction to Miss Bennet was beyond what I had ever seen in him before. I also watched your sister. Her look and manner were open, cheerful and pleasing as ever, but I saw no sign of strong feeling. If *you* have not been mistaken here, I must have been deceived. Your greater knowledge of your sister makes it probable that you were right.

My objections to the marriage were not only those which I mentioned last night in my own case. There were others. The inferiority of your mother's family, though a problem, was nothing compared with the total lack of good manners so frequently shown by herself, by your three younger sisters, and occasionally even by your father. Pardon me − it pains me to offend you. Let it be of comfort to you that the behaviour of yourself and your older sister has been so honourably free from such faults.

The anxiety of Bingley's sisters had been excited as much as my own. The action that followed is known to you. But I do not suppose that the marriage would have been prevented if I had not persuaded Bingley that your sister did not care for him. He believed me when I told him that he had deceived himself.

I cannot blame myself for having done this. There is only one point on which I feel some discomfort, and that is that I purposely deceived him by hiding from him the fact of your sister's being in town.

With regard to that other charge, of having done harm to Mr Wickham, I can only defend myself by telling the whole story. Mr Wickham was the son of my father's manager, a respectable man. My father had the son well educated, and, hoping that the church would be his profession, intended to provide for him in it. I, as a young man of about the same age, very soon realized that he had a bad character, a fact which he carefully hid from my father. Before he died, my father asked me to encourage his development, and, if he joined the church, to let him have a valuable family living. Shortly afterwards, Mr Wickham wrote to say that he had decided against becoming a minister. He wished instead to study law, and demanded money to help him. I willingly gave him this, knowing that he was not fit for the church, and he then in return gave up all claim to any appointment in it. Later, the position became free, and, having neglected his studies of the law and lived a life of laziness, he demanded it, and I refused.

Last summer he again most painfully forced himself on my notice. I must now mention a family matter that I would myself wish to forget, and which only present necessity causes me to make known to you. I feel quite confident of your ability to keep my secret.

My sister, who is ten years younger than I am, had just left school, and was placed in the care of a lady in Ramsgate. My trust in this woman was not well judged. She allowed Wickham, whom she knew, to make love to my sister, who agreed to run away with him. I went down to see her just before the intended flight. Georgiana was ashamed, and told me everything. You may imagine what I felt, and how I acted.

Wickham's chief object was, without doubt, my sister's fortune, which is thirty thousand pounds, but I cannot help supposing that he also hoped to annoy me.

Colonel Fitzwilliam will bear witness to the truth of everything that I have written here. I shall try to find some opportunity of putting this letter into your hands during the morning.

Sincerely,

FITZWILLIAM DARCY.

As Elizabeth eagerly read the letter, she experienced every kind of feeling. She began with a strong prejudice against whatever it might contain, and wished to disbelieve completely all the explanations that it put forward. She repeatedly told herself: 'This must be false! This cannot be!' When she had gone through the whole document, she put it away, promising herself that she would never look at it again.

But she could not do that. In half a minute the letter was unfolded again. She read and reread, with the closest attention, the details about Wickham. Of the two men concerned, one was free from blame, the other worthless. But how to decide between them? She tried to remember some example of goodness on Wickham's side. She could find none. He had pleased her by his appearance, his voice and his manner, but she knew nothing about his real character. The story of his intentions regarding Miss Darcy received some support from her conversation with Colonel Fitzwilliam only the morning before, and, according to Darcy, the Colonel would support every detail of this story.

She perfectly remembered everything that had passed in conversation between Wickham and herself during their first evening at Mr Philips's. Many of his expressions were still fresh in her memory. She was now struck with the bad taste of such remarks made to a stranger, and was surprised that it had escaped her notice before. She saw the lack of good breeding in the way in which he had put himself forward. She remembered that he had claimed to have no fear of seeing Mr Darcy, but he had avoided the Netherfield ball the very next week. She remembered also that until the Netherfield family had left the area, he had told his story to no one but herself, but after their removal he had discussed it freely, although he had told her that respect for the father would always prevent him from making public the injustice that was done to him by the son.

She became completely ashamed of herself. She felt that she had been blind, prejudiced, unreasonable.

She read again the part of the letter about Jane and was forced to admit to herself the justice of Darcy's description of her sister. She knew that Jane's feelings, though strong, were usually well hidden.

When she came to the part in which her family were

mentioned, in words so wounding to her pride but still so just in the blame that they expressed, her sense of shame was severe. The praise of herself and her sister was not unfelt, but it could not comfort her, and when she considered that Jane's disappointment had, in fact, been the work of her nearest relations, she felt in lower spirits than she had ever been before.

She soon began to know much of the letter by heart. She studied every sentence, and her feelings towards its writer were at times widely different. When she remembered the manner in which he had addressed her, she was still full of anger, but when she considered how unfairly she had misjudged him, her anger was turned against herself, and his disappointed feelings became the object of pity. She could feel grateful for his attachment and could respect his general character, but she could not approve of him, or be sorry about her refusal, or feel the slightest desire ever to see him again. In her own past behaviour, there was a continual cause for annoyance, and in the faults of her family, a subject of even heavier sorrow. They would never be put right. Her father, happy to laugh at them, would never trouble himself to control the wild foolishness of his youngest daughters, and her mother, with manners so far from perfect herself, was completely unconscious of the evil. Elizabeth had frequently united with Jane in an attempt to control the silliness of Kitty and Lydia, but while they were encouraged by their mother's fond carelessness, what chance could there be of improvement? Kitty, weak-spirited, nervous, and completely under Lydia's influence, had always been offended by their advice, and Lydia, careless and determined to have her own way, would hardly give them a hearing. They were foolish, lazy and empty-headed. While there was an officer in Meryton, they would be trying to attract him, and while Meryton was within walking distance of Longbourn, they would be going there for ever.

Anxiety for Jane was another cause of concern, and Mr

Darcy's explanation, by bringing back all her former good opinion of Bingley, increased the sense of what Jane had lost.

It may easily be believed that the events of the last two days had such an effect on Elizabeth's naturally happy spirits that she found it almost impossible to appear even reasonably cheerful. It was with a ready heart that she watched her visit to Hunsford come to an end in the next week. Mr Darcy had, she knew, left shortly after handing her the letter.

At last the boxes were packed, and the goodbyes over, not without a long speech from Mr Collins. The carriage drove off towards London, where Jane was to join the party for home.

'Oh!' cried Maria, after a few minutes' silence. 'It seems only a day or two since we first came! But so many things have happened!'

'A great many,' said her companion sadly.

'We had dinner nine times at Rosings, besides drinking tea there twice! How much I shall have to tell!'

Elizabeth privately added, 'And how much I shall have to hide!'

Chapter 16   Elizabeth and Jane Return Home

It was the second week in May when Jane, Elizabeth and Maria set out from London together for Hertfordshire, and as they came near the small hotel where Mr Bennet's carriage would meet them, they saw both Kitty and Lydia looking out of an upstairs room. These two girls had been in the place for more than an hour, happily employed in visiting a hat shop opposite and arranging a meal.

After welcoming their sisters, they proudly pointed to a table laid out with cold meat, crying, 'Isn't this nice? Isn't it a pleasant surprise?'

'And we want all of you to be our guests,' added Lydia, 'but you must lend us the money, because we have just spent ours at the shop over there.' Then, showing the things that she had bought: 'Look here, I have bought this hat. I don't think that it is very pretty, but I thought I might as well buy it as not. I shall pull it to pieces as soon as I get home, and remake it.'

And when her sisters criticized it as ugly, she added, 'It will not much matter what one wears this summer, as the regiment is leaving Meryton in two weeks' time.'

'Are they, really?' cried Elizabeth, with the greatest satisfaction.

'They are going to be camped near Brighton, and I do so want our father to take us all there for the summer! Mother would like to go, too, of all things!'

'Yes,' thought Elizabeth, '*that* would be pleasant. Oh, heavens! Brighton and a whole campful of soldiers, to us, who have been troubled enough already by one small regiment and the monthly dances at Meryton!'

'Now I have some news,' said Lydia, as they sat down at the table. 'It is excellent news about a person whom we all like.'

Jane and Elizabeth looked at each other, and the waiter was told that he need not stay. Lydia laughed, and said:

'Why must you always be so formal and correct? You thought that the waiter must not hear, as if he cared! But he is an ugly man! I am glad that he has gone. Well, but now for my news. It is about dear Wickham. There is no danger of his marrying Mary King. She has gone away. Wickham is safe.'

'And Mary King is safe!' added Elizabeth. 'Safe from a marriage which would be unwise in regard to fortune.'

As soon as everyone had eaten, and the older ones had paid, the carriage was ordered and the whole party, with their boxes, needlework bags and packages, and the unwelcome addition of all Kitty's and Lydia's shopping, were seated in it.

'How nicely we are packed in!' cried Lydia. 'Now let us be quite comfortable, and talk and laugh all the way home. And in the first place, let us hear what has happened to you all since you went away. Have you seen any pleasant men? I was in great hopes that one of you would have got a husband before you came back. Jane is almost twenty-three! How ashamed I should be of not being married before that age! Oh, how I should like to be married before any of you!'

In this noisy manner, with the help of Kitty, Lydia tried to amuse her companions all the way to Longbourn. Elizabeth listened as little as she could, but there was no escaping the frequent mention of Wickham's name.

Their welcome home was most kind. Mrs Bennet was glad to see Jane as beautiful as ever, and more than once Mr Bennet said to Elizabeth: 'I am glad that you have come back, Lizzy.'

Their party was large, as almost all the Lucases came to meet Maria and hear the news. Lady Lucas was inquiring of Maria, across the table, after the health and housekeeping affairs of her oldest daughter. Mrs Bennet was doubly engaged, on the one hand collecting an account of the present London fashions from Jane, who sat some way below her, and, on the other, repeating them all to the younger Miss Lucases. Lydia, in a voice rather louder than anyone else's, was describing the various pleasures of the morning to anybody who would listen to her.

'Oh, Mary,' she said, 'I wish you had gone with us! We had such fun! We talked and laughed so loudly that anybody might have heard us 10 miles away!'

To this, Mary replied, 'Do not think, my dear sister, that I scorn such pleasures. But I admit that they have no attraction for me. I would much prefer a book.'

But Lydia heard not a word of this answer. She rarely listened to anybody for more than half a minute, and never attended to Mary at all.

In the afternoon, Lydia was anxious for the other girls to walk to Meryton, but Elizabeth steadily opposed the suggestion. It should not be said that the Misses Bennet could not be at home half a day before they were in search of the officers. She did not want to see Wickham again, and was determined to avoid doing so for as long as possible.

♦

Elizabeth's impatience to inform Jane of what had happened could no longer be controlled, and at last, having decided to keep back every detail with which her sister was concerned, and having warned her to be surprised, she described to her the next morning most of the scene between Mr Darcy and herself. She then spoke of the letter, repeating all that it contained which mentioned George Wickham. What a blow this was for poor Jane, who would willingly have gone through the world without believing that so much evil existed in the whole human race, as was collected here in one person.

'I do not know when I have been more shocked,' she said. 'Wickham so very bad! It is almost beyond belief. And poor Mr Darcy! Dear Lizzy, only consider what he must have suffered! Such a disappointment, and with the knowledge of your bad opinion too! And having to tell such a thing about his sister!'

'There is one point on which I want your advice. I want to be told whether I ought or ought not to make known the truth about Wickham's character to our friends in general.'

Miss Bennet thought a little, and then replied, 'Surely there can be no reason for shaming him so terribly. What is your own opinion?'

'That it ought not to be attempted. Mr Darcy has not given me permission to make his information public. At present I will say nothing about it.'

'You are quite right. It might ruin him for ever, if his past became known. He is now, perhaps, sorry for what he has done, and anxious to improve.'

The confusion in Elizabeth's mind was relieved by this conversation. She had got rid of two of the secrets which had weighed on her for two weeks, and was certain of a willing listener in Jane whenever she might want to talk again of either. But she dared not tell the other half of Mr Darcy's letter, nor explain to her sister how sincerely she had been valued by his friend. Here was knowledge which no one could share.

She now had time to observe the real state of her sister's spirits. Jane was not happy. She still had very warm feelings for Bingley.

'Well, Lizzy,' said Mrs Bennet one day, 'what is your opinion now of this sad business of Jane's?'

'I do not think that Mr Bingley will ever live at Netherfield again.'

'Oh, well! It is just as he chooses. Well, my comfort is, I am sure that Jane will die of a broken heart, and then he will be sorry for what he has done.'

But as Elizabeth could not receive comfort from any such expectations, she did not answer.

'Well, Lizzy,' her mother continued, soon afterwards, 'and so the Collinses live very comfortably, do they? Charlotte is an excellent manager, I expect. If she is half as sharp as her mother, she is saving enough. And I suppose they often talk of having Longbourn when your father is dead. They look on it quite as their own, I dare say. I would be ashamed of owning somewhere that was left me on such unjust conditions.'

Chapter 17   The Regiment Leaves Meryton

The second week of their return was the last of the regiment's stay in Meryton, and all the young ladies in the neighbourhood were in the lowest of spirits. Only the older Misses Bennet were still able to eat, drink and sleep, and to continue the usual course of their lives. Very frequently they were charged with heartlessness by Kitty and Lydia, whose own unhappiness was extreme.

'Heavens! What will become of us?' they would often cry in bitterness. 'How can you be smiling so, Lizzy?' Their fond mother shared all their unhappiness. She remembered what she had suffered on a similar occasion in her youth.

'I am sure,' she said, 'that I cried for two days when Colonel Millar's regiment went away. I thought that my heart would break.'

'I am sure that *mine* will break,' said Lydia.

'If only we could go to Brighton,' said Mrs Bennet.

'Oh, yes! But Father is so disagreeable.'

Such were the complaints continually repeated at Longbourn House. Elizabeth tried to be amused by them, but all sense of pleasure was lost in shame. She felt once more the justice of Mr Darcy's criticisms, and she had never been so ready to pardon his part in the affairs of his friend.

But the darkness of Lydia's future was lightened shortly afterwards. She received an invitation from Mrs Forster, the wife of the colonel of the regiment, to go with her to Brighton. This friend was a young woman, and very recently married.

The joy of Lydia on this occasion, the pleasure of Mrs Bennet, and the jealous anger of Kitty, are hardly to be described. Without any concern for her sister's feelings, Lydia flew about the house in restless excitement, calling for everybody's congratulations, and laughing and talking with more violence than ever, while the luckless Kitty continued to complain.

'I cannot see why Mrs Forster did not ask me as well as Lydia,' she said, 'I have just as much right to be asked as she has, and more, too, because I am two years older.'

Elizabeth tried to make her more reasonable, and Jane urged her to bear her disappointment quietly, but without success. As for Elizabeth herself, she considered this invitation as the deathblow to any possibility of common sense in Lydia, and, though such an act would make her hated if it became known, she could not help secretly advising her father not to let her go. She suggested to him the probability of Lydia's being even more foolish with such a companion at Brighton, where the opportunities for silliness must be greater than at home.

'If you knew,' said Elizabeth, 'of the very great disadvantage which has already come from the public notice of Lydia's uncontrolled behaviour, I am sure that you would judge it unwise to let her go.'

'Already come!' repeated Mr Bennet. 'What! Has she frightened away some of your lovers? Poor little Lizzy! But do not be disheartened. Young men who cannot bear to be connected with a little silliness are not worth worrying over.'

But Elizabeth, excusing herself for speaking so plainly to her father, continued in her attempt to persuade him of the growing lack of self-control that both his younger daughters showed in public, and the danger of their characters becoming fixed. He saw that her whole heart was in the subject and, taking her hand warmly, said in reply:

'Do not make yourself anxious, my love. Wherever you and Jane are known, you must be respected and valued, and you will not appear to less advantage because you have a pair of – or I may say, three – very silly sisters. We shall have no peace at home if Lydia does not go to Brighton. Let her go, then. Colonel Forster is a sensible man, and will keep her from any real harm, and she is luckily too poor to attract any fortune-hunters. At Brighton she will be of less importance than here. Let us hope, therefore, that it may teach her a little about life.'

With this answer Elizabeth was forced to be satisfied.

♦

Elizabeth now saw Wickham for the last time. Having met him frequently since her return, she had become fairly well used to the situation. Her interest in him had quite gone, and in his present behaviour to herself she had a fresh cause for displeasure. The readiness that he soon showed in renewing his attentions to her, now that Miss King had gone, proved that he judged her to be foolish enough to be pleased by notice from him at any time that he chose to give it.

On the very last day of the regiment's stay he had dinner, with some other officers at Longbourn. Elizabeth was so unwilling to part from him in a friendly way that she mentioned the fact that Colonel Fitzwilliam and Mr Darcy had both spent three weeks at Rosings, and asked him whether he was acquainted with the former.

He looked surprised, displeased, anxious; but, controlling himself, soon replied that he had formerly seen him often, and asked how she liked him. She answered warmly in his favour, and went on to say that from knowing Mr Darcy better, he, too, was better understood and liked.

Wickham's anxiety now appeared in a reddened face and a troubled look. He did not dare to say much more, but in spite of an appearance of cheerfulness, it was clear that he would now be glad to leave the area.

When the party ended, Lydia returned with Mrs Forster to Meryton, from which place they would set out early the next morning. The separation between her and her family was noisy rather than painful. Kitty was the only one to cry, and her tears were from jealousy and from pity for herself. In the loud happiness of Lydia herself in saying goodbye, the more gentle last words of her sisters were spoken without being heard.

Chapter 18   Pemberley

Mr Bennet's marriage had been the result of a lack of good judgment. Attracted by youth and beauty, and that appearance of good temper which they usually give, he had married a woman whose weak understanding and narrow mind had very soon put an end to real love for her. Respect and confidence had gone for ever, and his hopes of happiness at home were ended. But he was fond of the country and of books, and his wife's foolishness and lack of knowledge gave him amusement.

Elizabeth had never been blind to the unfitting nature of her father's behaviour as a husband. It had always upset her, but, respecting his abilities and grateful for his caring treatment of herself, she had tried to forget what she could not fail to notice. But she had never felt so strongly as now the disadvantages that must be experienced by the children of so unsuitable a marriage.

When Lydia went away, she promised to write very often and in great detail to her mother and Kitty, but her letters were always long expected and very short. Those to her mother contained little but unimportant news, and those to Kitty, though longer, contained too many secrets to be read to the family.

Life in Meryton was undoubtedly duller after the regiment had left. Elizabeth began to look forward to her northern tour with her aunt and uncle, the date of which was approaching. Her disappointment was therefore great when she learnt that business prevented her uncle from being away from London as long as he had hoped. They were forced to give up the visit to the Lakes, and to choose a shorter tour; according to the present plan, they were to go no further north than Derbyshire, where Mrs Gardiner hoped to revisit the town in which she had spent the earlier part of her life. There were many ideas connected in Elizabeth's mind with the mention of Derbyshire. It was impossible for her to see or hear the word without thinking of Pemberley and its owner.

♦

At last the period of waiting was over, and Mr and Mrs Gardiner, with their four children, appeared at Longbourn. The children, two girls of six and eight years old, and two younger boys, would be left in the special care of their cousin Jane, who was the favourite, and whose steady good sense and sweetness of temper exactly suited her for looking after them in every way – teaching them, playing with them, and loving them.

The Gardiners stayed at Longbourn for only one night, and set out the next morning with Elizabeth on their travels. One enjoyment was certain – that of pleasure in each other's company.

Their journey took them to many interesting and well-known places – Oxford, Blenheim, Warwick, Kenilworth, and others. At last, after having seen all the chief sights of the area, they continued on their way to the little town of Lambton in Derbyshire, the scene of Mrs Gardiner's former home, and Elizabeth found that Pemberley was only 5 miles away from Lambton. In talking over their plans, Mrs Gardiner expressed a wish to see the place again. Mr Gardiner expressed his willingness, and their niece was asked for her approval.

Elizabeth was in an awkward situation. She felt that she had no business at Pemberley, and she pretended, therefore, that she was tired of seeing great houses. Mrs Gardiner thought this stupid, and Elizabeth did not know what to do. The possibility of meeting Mr Darcy was frightening. She trembled at the very idea. Fortunately, she was able to find out from a servant at the hotel where they were staying that Pemberley's owner was absent, so when the subject was mentioned again the next morning, she readily agreed, because her unwillingness had turned to interest.

As they drove along, Elizabeth's mind was too full for conversation, but she saw and admired every notable view. The park was very large, and they passed through a beautiful wood stretching over a wide area. Pemberley House was a large, fine-looking stone building, on ground slightly higher than the park; in front, a stream had been widened without making it appear at all artificial. Elizabeth had never seen a place for which nature had done so much, or where natural beauty had been so little spoilt by awkward taste. Her aunt and uncle were equally warm in their admiration, and at that moment she felt that there were in fact advantages to being the lady of Pemberley!

On arriving at the house, they were admitted to the hall. The housekeeper was a respectable-looking woman, who showed them round the chief rooms. From every window there were beauties to be seen. The rooms themselves were of good height and fine shape, and with furniture in excellent taste.

'I might have been the lady of this place,' she thought. 'Instead of viewing it as a stranger, I might have been welcoming my aunt and uncle as my guests. But no,' she remembered, 'I would not have been allowed to invite my relations.'

This was a lucky thought – it saved her from feeling sorry for herself.

She wished very much to inquire of the housekeeper whether her master was really absent. At last the question was asked by her uncle, and she turned away anxiously when the reply came, 'We expect him tomorrow, with a large party of friends.'

Her aunt now called her to look at a picture, and asked her with a smile how she liked it. It was of Wickham. The housekeeper mentioned his name, and added, 'He has now gone into the army, but I am afraid that he has turned out very wild.'

Mrs Gardiner looked at her niece with a smile, but Elizabeth could not return it.

They then looked at pictures of Mr Darcy and his sister.

'And is Miss Darcy as good-looking as her brother?' said Mr Gardiner.

'Oh, yes,' replied the housekeeper, 'the best-looking young lady that ever was seen, and so skilled! She plays and sings the whole day long. In the next room there is a new instrument that has just arrived for her – a present from my master. She is coming here tomorrow with him.'

'Does your master spend much time at Pemberley?'

'Not as much as I would wish, sir. Miss Darcy is always here for the summer months.'

'Except,' thought Elizabeth, 'when she goes to Ramsgate.'

'If your master married, you might see more of him.'

'Yes, sir, but I do not know who is good enough for him.'

Mr and Mrs Gardiner smiled.

'I say no more than the truth. I have never had an angry word from him in my life, and I have known him ever since he was four years old.'

Elizabeth's keenest attention was excited. This was praise of the strongest kind, and most opposite to her ideas.

'He is the best master that ever lived. Some people call him proud, but I never saw anything of it.'

Mr Gardiner was highly amused as she continued to describe the good qualities of her master. He judged that her extreme praise of him was the result of family prejudice.

'This fine account of him,' whispered Mrs Gardiner to her niece, 'does not agree with his behaviour to our poor friend.'

Elizabeth said rather quietly that they might have been deceived.

'That is not very likely. Our information was *too* direct.'

They were then shown into a very pretty little sitting room with new furniture, and were told that it was done just to give pleasure to Miss Darcy, who had become fond of the room when last at Pemberley.

'It is always the way with him,' the housekeeper explained. 'Whatever can give his sister pleasure is sure to be done.'

'He is a good brother,' said Elizabeth.

There was certainly at this moment in her mind a more gentle feeling towards him than she had ever had when she was closely acquainted with him. Every idea brought forward by the housekeeper was favourable to his character, and as she looked once again at his picture, she felt more grateful to him for his good opinion of her than she had ever done before.

◆

The house had now been examined, and they went outside in the charge of the gardener to admire the grounds. As they walked towards the river, Elizabeth turned back to look again, and as she did so, the owner of the building suddenly came forward from the road that led behind it.

They were within 20 yards of each other, and his appearance was so sudden that it was impossible to avoid him. Their eyes met immediately. He stopped, and then for a moment seemed unable to move from surprise. Quickly recovering his self-control, though, he walked towards the party and spoke to Elizabeth, if not with perfect calm, at least with perfect politeness.

She had immediately turned away, but when he approached she received his greetings with a confusion that it was impossible to control. Mr and Mrs Gardiner stood a little way off while he was talking to their niece, who, shocked by their meeting, hardly dared lift her eyes to his face and did not know what answer she returned to his polite inquiries after her family. She was full of surprise at the change in his manner since they last parted, and found that every sentence that he spoke was increasing her confusion. As the realization of the awkwardness of her being found there returned to her mind, the few minutes in which they were together were some of the most uncomfortable in her life. He did not seem less shocked. When he spoke, his voice had none of its usual calmness, and he repeated some of his questions more than once.

At last, every idea seemed to fail him and, after standing for a few minutes without saying a word, he suddenly went away. The others then joined her. Elizabeth was filled with shame and annoyance. Her coming there was the most unfortunate, most unwise thing in the world! How shameful it must appear to a man who thought so highly of himself! It might seem as if she had purposely put herself in his way again. Oh! Why had she come? Or why did he come a day before he was expected? And his behaviour, so noticeably changed – what could it mean? It was astonishing that he should ever speak to her – but to speak with such politeness, to inquire after her family! Never in her life had she seen him so gentle. She did not know what to think.

They now entered a beautiful walk by the water, but it was some time before Elizabeth could give it any attention, although she replied without thinking to the remarks of her companions. She greatly wished to know what was passing in Mr Darcy's mind, and whether, in spite of everything, she was still dear to him.

After wandering on for some time quite slowly, because Mrs Gardiner was not a great walker and was becoming tired, they were again surprised by the sight of Mr Darcy approaching them. Elizabeth saw that he had lost none of his recent politeness, and to show that she too could be polite, she began to admire the place. But she had not got beyond the word "beautiful", when some unlucky thought reminded her that praise of Pemberley might be misunderstood. The colour in her face deepened, and she said no more.

As she paused, he asked her if she would do him the honour of introducing him to her friends. This was quite unexpected. 'What will be his surprise,' she thought, 'when he knows who they are? He thinks that they are people of social position.'

The introduction, though, was made immediately, and as she named them as family relations of hers, she took a secret look at him to see how he bore it. It was plain that he was surprised, but instead of going away, he turned back with them and entered into conversation with Mr Gardiner. Elizabeth could not help being pleased. It was comforting that he should know that she had some relations of whom there was no need to be ashamed. She listened carefully, and felt happiness in every expression, every sentence of her uncle that showed his intelligence, his taste, or his good manners.

The conversation soon turned to fishing, and she heard Mr Darcy, with the greatest politeness, invite him to fish there as often as he chose. Mrs Gardiner, who was walking arm in arm with Elizabeth, gave her a look of surprise. Elizabeth said nothing, but she was extremely pleased. The mark of attention must be all for herself.

A little later, Mrs Gardiner, tired by the exercise of the morning, found Elizabeth's arm not strong enough to support her, and therefore preferred her husband's. Mr Darcy took her place by her niece. After a short silence, the lady spoke first. She wished him to know that she had been informed of his absence before she came to the place. He admitted that he had put forward his arrival because of some business. 'The rest of my party,' he continued, 'will be here tomorrow, and among them are some with whom you are acquainted – Mr Bingley and his sisters.'

Elizabeth answered only by a slight lowering of her head.

After a pause, he added: 'There is also a person who especially wishes to be known to you. Will you allow me, or do I ask too much, to introduce my sister to you?'

The surprise of such a request was great – too great for her to remember later in what manner she agreed. They now walked on in silence. Elizabeth was not comfortable – that was impossible – but she was pleased by his attention.

When Mr and Mrs Gardiner came up to them at the house, they were all urged to go inside and take some tea, but this was politely refused. Mr Darcy handed the ladies into the carriage, and when it drove off, Elizabeth saw him walking slowly towards the house.

Her uncle and aunt now began to speak very favourably of his effect on them. They were cross with her, saying, 'Why did you tell us he was so disagreeable?'

Elizabeth excused herself as well as she could.

She then felt it her duty to tell them, in as careful a manner as she could, that she believed herself to have been mistaken in thinking that he had been at fault in his treatment of Wickham. Mrs Gardiner was surprised, but as they were now approaching the scenes of her youth, all her interest was soon taken up by the pleasures of her memories, and the meeting after many years of old friends, so Elizabeth was set free from awkward questions, and could be left with her own thoughts.

Chapter 19   The Bingleys

Mr Darcy brought his sister to visit Elizabeth a few hours after her arrival the next day. The Gardiners were surprised again, and a new idea on the subject began to enter their heads.

Elizabeth saw with astonishment that the young lady with

whom she was now made acquainted was not extremely proud, as had been reported, but only extremely shy. The expression on her face showed sense and natural good temper, and her manners were perfectly gentle.

They had not been together long before Bingley also came to call on Elizabeth. His manner was unchanged, and he looked and spoke with friendly confidence. To Mr and Mrs Gardiner, who knew what he meant to Jane, he was hardly a less interesting person than to herself. The whole party excited their attention. They were taken up in observing Mr Darcy and their niece. They remained a little in doubt about the lady's feelings, but it was clear that the gentleman was overflowing with admiration.

Elizabeth, on her side, had much to do. She wished to be agreeable to her visitors. She was watching Bingley with Miss Darcy, who had been put forward as a competitor to Jane. She saw nothing in the behaviour of either that gave support to the words of Miss Bingley. In a voice of real sadness, Bingley observed to her, at a moment when the others were talking together, that they had not met for eight months, not since 26 November, when they were all dancing together at Netherfield. Elizabeth was pleased that his memory was so exact. He later took an opportunity to ask her privately whether *all* her sisters were at Longbourn. There was not much in the question, but his look and manner gave it meaning.

It was not often that she could turn her eyes on Mr Darcy himself, but when she did manage to look in his direction, she saw him doing his best to gain the good opinion of her relations, and when the visit came to an end, the wish was expressed of seeing them all at dinner at Pemberley two days later.

◆

It had been agreed between the aunt and the niece that such a striking piece of politeness as Miss Darcy's, in coming to see them on the very day of her arrival, ought to be returned, though it could not be equalled. It was therefore decided to call on her at Pemberley the following morning. Elizabeth was pleased, though when she asked herself the reason, she had very little to say in reply.

When they reached the house, they were received by Miss Darcy, who was sitting with Mrs Hurst and Miss Bingley and the lady with whom she lived in London. Georgiana's welcome was very shy, and might have given a false idea of pride, but Mrs Gardiner and her niece understood her difficulty and pitied her.

Mrs Hurst and Miss Bingley greeted them in few words, and when they were seated an awkward pause followed. It was broken by Miss Darcy's companion, a woman of good breeding, who carried on a conversation with Mrs Gardiner with some help from Elizabeth. Miss Darcy looked as if she wished for courage enough to join in.

Elizabeth soon saw that she was closely watched by Miss Bingley. After a quarter of an hour, Miss Bingley inquired coldly after the health of her family, and Elizabeth replied just as coldly.

Some servants then entered with cold meat, cake, and a variety of all the finest fruits in season, and soon after that Mr Darcy, who had been fishing with Mr Gardiner, made his appearance.

Elizabeth decided to appear perfectly calm and relaxed, especially when she realized that the suspicions of the whole party were causing close observation of every word, expression and movement from Darcy or herself. In no face was this so clearly expressed as in Miss Bingley's, in spite of the smiles that spread over it when she addressed one of them. Jealousy had not yet made her give up hope, and she still planned to win Mr Darcy. But a little later, in an unwise moment of anger, she said with scornful politeness:

'I believe, Miss Eliza, that the regiment has left Meryton. They must be a great loss to *your* family.'

Elizabeth answered calmly, and while she spoke, she noticed that the colour in Darcy's face had deepened, and that his sister was full of confusion. Miss Bingley little knew what pain she was giving her friend. She had only intended to anger Elizabeth, and make her show some feeling that might harm her in Darcy's opinion. Elizabeth's self-control soon lessened his discomfort, and as Miss Bingley, annoyed and disappointed, dared not move any closer to the subject of Wickham, Georgiana, too, recovered in time.

Their visit did not continue for long after this, and when Mr Darcy returned from walking them to their carriage, Miss Bingley was busy criticizing Elizabeth's appearance, behaviour and dress.

'How very ugly Eliza Bennet looks this morning!' she cried. 'I have never in my life seen anyone so much changed as she is since the winter. She has become so brown and rough-looking. I must admit, though, that I could never see any beauty in her. Her features are not at all attractive, and as for her eyes, they have a sharp look to them.'

As Miss Bingley believed that Mr Darcy admired Elizabeth, this was not the best way of persuading him that he should prefer her, but angry people are not always wise. He looked annoyed, but remained silent, and from a determination to make him speak, she continued:

'I remember, when we first knew her in Hertfordshire, how you yourself said one night, after they had been having dinner at Netherfield, "She, a beauty! I should as soon call her mother a person of high intelligence!" But I believe you thought her rather pretty afterwards.'

'Yes,' replied Darcy, who could no longer control himself. 'For many months I have considered her to be one of the best-looking women of my acquaintance.'

In the carriage, as they returned to their hotel, Mrs Gardiner and Elizabeth talked of all that had happened during their visit, except what particularly interested them both and the person who had attracted their attention most. They spoke of his sister, his friends, his house, his fruit, of everything except himself! But Elizabeth was anxious to know what Mrs Gardiner thought of him, and Mrs Gardiner would have been extremely pleased if her niece had introduced the subject!

Chapter 20   Lydia and Wickham

Elizabeth had been a good deal disappointed in not hearing from Jane on their arrival at Lambton, and this disappointment was renewed on both mornings that had now been spent there, but on the third her anxiety was relieved by receiving two letters together, of which the earlier one had been sent elsewhere because the address was not clearly written.

Her aunt and uncle set out on a walk, leaving her to enjoy them in quiet. The earlier one had been written five days before, and began with an account of their little parties and social events and unimportant local news, but the second half, which was dated a day later, gave more important information. It said:

Since writing yesterday, dearest Lizzy, something of a most unexpected and serious nature has happened. What I have to say concerns poor Lydia. An urgent message from Colonel Forster came at twelve last night, just as we had all gone to bed, to inform us that she had gone off to Scotland with one of his officers – to tell the truth, with Wickham! Imagine our surprise. But to Kitty it does not seem completely unexpected. I am very, very sorry. Such an unwise marriage on both sides! They went off on Saturday night at about twelve, but were not missed until yesterday morning. I must end this letter, because I cannot spend long away from my poor mother, who is sadly troubled. I am afraid that you will not be able to read this letter, for I hardly know what I have written.

Without allowing herself time for consideration, Elizabeth immediately seized the other letter and, opening it with the greatest impatience, read as follows:

By this time, my dearest sister, you will have received my hurried letter. I hope this will be clearer, but my head is so confused that I cannot be certain of it. Dearest Lizzy, I have bad news for you, and it cannot be delayed. Although a marriage between Mr Wickham and our poor Lydia would be very unwise, we are now anxious to be sure that the ceremony has actually been performed. Though Lydia left a short note for Mrs Forster giving her the idea that they were going to Gretna Green,* something that Denny said showed his belief that Wickham never intended to go there, or to marry Lydia at all. This was repeated to Colonel Forster, who immediately became anxious and set out in search of them. He managed to follow their course, but only as far as London, where they have disappeared. After making every possible inquiry, he kindly came on to Longbourn and told us the bad news.

Our anxiety, my dear Lizzy, is very great. My mother and father believe the worst has happened, but I cannot think so badly of Wickham. Perhaps they have some reason for being married privately in town. My poor mother is really ill, and as for my father, I never in my life saw him so troubled. Poor Kitty has to bear our parents' anger for having hidden the nature of their friendship, but as it was a matter of confidence, one cannot be

*Gretna Green: a place in Scotland where young people could marry quickly and without their parent's permission.

surprised that she did so. I am truly glad, dearest Lizzy, that you have been saved from some of these scenes, but now that the first shock is over, shall I admit that I greatly wish for your return? But I am not so unkind as to urge it, if it is inconvenient. My father is going to London immediately to try to discover Lydia, but the extreme state of his feelings will not allow him to act in the wisest way. At a time like this, my uncle's advice and help would be everything in the world.

'Oh, where, where is my uncle?' cried Elizabeth, jumping from her seat as she finished the letter, in eagerness to follow him without loss of time. But as she reached the door, it was opened by a servant, and Mr Darcy appeared. Her pale face and hurried manner struck him immediately, and before he could recover from his surprise, she quickly said, 'I beg your pardon, but I must leave you. I must find Mr Gardiner this moment on business that cannot be delayed.'

'Oh, heavens! What is the matter?' he cried, with more feeling than politeness. Then, calming himself, he added, 'I will not keep you a minute, but let me, or let the servant, go after Mr Gardiner. You are not well enough. You cannot go yourself.'

Elizabeth paused, but her knees trembled under her and, calling back the servant, she gave him the message. When he had left the room, she sat down, unable to support herself, and looked so ill and unhappy that it was impossible for Darcy to leave her, or to prevent himself from saying, in a voice of gentleness and sympathy, 'Let me call a woman for you. Is there nothing you could take to give yourself some relief? Shall I get you a glass of wine? You are very ill.'

'No, I thank you,' she replied, trying to recover herself. 'I am quite well. I am only anxious about some terrible news from home.'

She burst into tears as she mentioned it, and for a few minutes could not speak another word. Finally she went on, 'My youngest sister has left all her friends – has run away – has thrown herself into the power of – of Mr Wickham. She has no money, nothing that he could want – she is ruined for ever.'

Darcy stood still with astonishment.

'When I consider,' Elizabeth added, 'that I might have prevented it! I, who knew what he really was. But it is too late!'

Darcy quietly expressed his sympathy, and Elizabeth, in answer to his inquiries, told him what details she knew. He hardly seemed to hear her, and was walking up and down in deep thought, with a serious and troubled expression on his face. Elizabeth immediately understood. Her power over him was sinking under such a proof of family weakness, such a certainty of the deepest dishonour. She could neither blame him, nor feel any surprise, but the situation was exactly of a kind to make her understand her own wishes, and she had never so honestly felt that she could have loved him as now, when all love must be without hope.

But her own troubles were soon swallowed up in the memory of Lydia and, covering her face with her hands, she was soon lost to everything else. After a pause of several minutes, she was brought back to the present situation by the voice of her companion, who said, 'This unfortunate affair will, I fear, prevent my sister's having the pleasure of seeing you at Pemberley today.'

'Oh, yes! Please be kind enough to apologize for us to Miss Darcy. Say that urgent business calls us home. Hide the truth as long as possible.'

He agreed to do so and, with only one serious parting look, went away. As he left the room, Elizabeth felt how improbable it was that they should ever see each other again in such a friendly way. Looking back over the whole of their acquaintance, so full of differences and variety, she felt saddened at the awkward change in her feelings, which would now have encouraged its continuance, and would formerly have been glad at its ending.

If grateful feelings and respect form part of love, Elizabeth's change of feelings will be considered neither improbable nor faulty. The fact is certain that she saw him go with sadness and found additional pain in this early example of what Lydia's behaviour must produce. She had no hope of Wickham meaning to marry her sister. She had never noticed, while the regiment was in Meryton, that Lydia had any special liking for him, but she was sure that Lydia only needed encouragement to form a strong relationship with anybody. Sometimes one officer, sometimes another had been her favourite. Though she did not suppose Lydia to be purposely running away without the intention of marriage, she believed that she would easily be tricked by a deceitful man.

Mr and Mrs Gardiner had hurried back, worried, and Elizabeth told them the cause of her message. Although Lydia had never been a favourite with them, they could not help being deeply shocked. After they had expressed their feelings of sympathy, Mr Gardiner promised every help that it was in his power to give, and everything concerning their journey was speedily arranged.

'But what is to be done about Pemberley?' cried Mrs Gardiner.

'I told Mr Darcy that we should not be able to go there tonight. That is all settled.'

'What is all settled?' repeated Mrs Gardiner to herself, as she ran to her room to get herself ready for travelling. 'And do they know each other so well that she can tell him the real truth? How I wish that I knew!'

Packing had to be done, and notes had to be written to all their friends in Lambton, with excuses for their leaving so suddenly. An hour, though, was enough to complete everything, and at the end of that hour Elizabeth found herself seated in the carriage, on the road to Longbourn.

Chapter 21   Mr Gardiner Goes to London

They travelled as quickly as possible, and, having slept one night on the way, reached Longbourn by dinnertime the next day.

The little Gardiners, attracted by the sight of the carriage, were standing on the steps of the house, and the joyful surprise that lit up their faces was the travellers' first welcome.

Elizabeth jumped out, gave each of them a quick kiss, and hurried into the hall, where Jane, who came running downstairs from her mother's room, met her immediately.

As Elizabeth greeted her warmly, tears filled the eyes of both sisters. The younger, though, did not lose a moment before asking whether anything had been heard of the missing pair.

'Not yet,' replied Jane.

'Is our father in town?'

'Yes, he went on Tuesday.'

'And have you heard from him often?'

'Only once, to say that he had arrived and to give me his address. He only added that he would not write again until he had something important to mention.'

'And our mother – how is she?'

'Fairly well, though her nerves are troubling her a great deal, and she is still in bed. Mary and Kitty, thank heaven, are quite well.'

'But you – how are you?' cried Elizabeth. 'You look pale. How much you must have suffered!'

Her sister told her that she was perfectly well, and their conversation, which had been continued while Mr and Mrs Gardiner were with their children, was now ended by the approach of the whole party.

Mrs Bennet, to whose room they all went, received them exactly as might be expected, with tears and expressions of sadness, angry words against Wickham, and complaints of her own sufferings. She blamed everybody but the person who, by bringing up her daughter so carelessly, was chiefly responsible for her faults.

'If I had been able,' she said, 'to go to Brighton with all my family, *this* would never have happened – but poor dear Lydia had no one to look after her. Poor dear child! And now here's Mr Bennet gone away, and I know he'll fight Wickham, and then he'll be killed, and what will become of us all? The Collinses will turn us out before he is cold in his grave and if you are not kind to us, brother, I do not know what we shall do.'

They all comforted her against such terrible ideas, and Mr Gardiner told her that he would go directly to London and give Mr Bennet every help in his search.

'Oh, my dear brother,' replied Mrs Bennet, 'that is exactly what I could most wish for. And now do, when you get to town, find them, wherever they may be, and if they are not already married, *make* them marry. And as for clothes for the wedding, do not let them wait for that, but tell Lydia that she shall have as much money as she chooses to buy them, after they are married. And above all things, keep Mr Bennet from fighting. Tell him what a terrible state I am in – that I am frightened to death, and have such tremblings all over me, and such pains in my head, and such beatings of my heart that I can get no rest by night or by day. And tell my dear Lydia not to give any orders about her clothes until she has seen me, because she does not know the best shops. Oh, brother, how kind you are! I know that you will manage everything.'

Mr Gardiner could not avoid advising her not to be extreme, in her hopes as well as her fears, and the conversation continued in this manner until dinner was on the table and they left her to the attentions of the housekeeper.

Although Mr and Mrs Gardiner were sure that there was no real necessity for her to stay in bed, they did not attempt to oppose her desire, because they knew that she had not enough good sense to keep quiet while the servants were around.

They were joined by Mary and Kitty, who had been too busy in their separate rooms to make their appearance before. The one came from her books, the other from the business of dressing herself. They were both fairly calm, and no change was noticeable in either, except that the loss of her favourite sister, or the anger which she herself had had to bear in the matter, had made Kitty more complaining than usual.

In the afternoon, the two older Misses Bennet were able to have half an hour by themselves in serious talk. Elizabeth learnt that Wickham's bad character had begun to be known. Colonel Forster believed him to be a careless and wasteful spender, and it was now said that he had left Meryton greatly in debt.

'Oh, Jane, if we had been less secretive, if we had told what we knew of him, this could not have happened.'

'We acted with the best intentions.'

Jane then showed Elizabeth Lydia's letter to Mrs Forster, which the Colonel had brought with him. This is what it contained:

My dear Harriet,

You will laugh when you know where I have gone, and I cannot help laughing myself at your surprise tomorrow morning, as soon as I am missed. I am going to Gretna Green, and if you cannot guess with whom, I shall think you very stupid, because there is only one man in the world that I love, and he is perfect. I could never be happy without him, so I think it will do no harm to run away with him. You need not tell them at Longbourn if you do not want to, because it will make the surprise much greater when I write to them and sign my name Lydia Wickham. What a good joke it will be! Please make my excuses to Pratt for not keeping my promise to dance with him tonight. I shall send for my clothes when I get to Longbourn, but I wish you would tell the servant to mend a great hole in my blue dress before it is packed. Goodbye. Give my love to Colonel Forster. I hope that you will drink to our good journey.

Your loving friend,

LYDIA BENNET.

'Oh, thoughtless, thoughtless Lydia!' cried Elizabeth when she had finished reading. 'What a letter this is to be written at such a moment! But at least it shows that she was serious in the object of her journey. My poor father! How he must have felt!'

'I never saw anyone so shocked. He could not speak a word for fully ten minutes. Our mother was taken ill immediately, and the whole house was in confusion.'

'Oh, Jane,' cried Elizabeth, 'was there one servant belonging to us who did not know the whole story before the end of the day?'

'I do not know. I hope so. But it is very difficult to be careful at such a time.'

'You do not look well. You have had every care and anxiety to bear by yourself.'

'Mary and Kitty have been very kind, and would have shared every duty, I am sure, but Kitty is thin and delicate, and Mary studies so much that she should not be interrupted during her hours of rest. Our Aunt Philips came to us after our father had gone away, and was of great use and comfort, and Lady Lucas has been very kind, and walked over here to offer her sympathy and help.'

'It would have been better if she had stayed at home,' cried Elizabeth. 'Perhaps she meant well, but in a time of such a misfortune as this, one cannot see too little of one's neighbours.'

Chapter 22   Mr Bennet Returns

All Meryton now seemed eager to speak badly of the man who, only three months before, had been considered to be the perfect gentleman. He was said to be in debt to every shopkeeper in the place, and to have made love to most of their daughters. Everybody spoke of him as the worst young man in the world, and everybody began to find out that they had always distrusted the appearance of his goodness.

Mrs Philips visited the Bennets frequently with the intention, she said, of cheering them up, but as she never came without reporting some fresh example of his wrongdoings, she rarely went away without leaving them in lower spirits than she had found them.

Every day at Longbourn was now a day of anxiety, but the most anxious part of each was when the post was expected. Still no news of any importance came from London, but a letter arrived for their father from a different direction, from Mr Collins. As Jane had been told by Mr Bennet to open everything that came for him in his absence, she read it, and Elizabeth, who knew how strange Mr Collins's letters always were, looked over her shoulder and read it too.

My dear Sir,

I feel it is my duty, as a relative of yours, and because of my situation in life, to sympathize with you in your present misfortune, which must be of the bitterest kind, since it stems from a cause that no time can remove. The death of your daughter would have been a relief in comparison with this. It is all the worse, because I understand there is reason to suppose that this behaviour of your daughter was caused by a lack of rules at home, though at the same time I suspect that her character must be naturally bad. In any case, you are greatly to be pitied, in which opinion I am joined not only by my wife, but also by Lady Catherine and her daughter. They agree with me that this foolish act will harm the fortunes of all your other daughters, for who will connect themselves with such a family? This consideration leads me to think with increased satisfaction of a certain event of last November, for if it had been otherwise, I should have shared all your sorrow and shame. Let me advise you, my dear sir, to throw off your ungrateful child for ever, and leave her to the fruits of her wrongdoings.

I am, dear sir, etc.

At last, after the failure of all attempts to find his daughter, Mr Bennet agreed to Mr Gardiner's request that he should return to his family and leave it to him to do whatever seemed advisable. When Mrs Bennet was told of this, she did not express as much satisfaction as her children expected.

'What! Is he coming home, and without poor Lydia? Who is to fight Wickham and make him marry her, if he comes away?'

As Mrs Gardiner began to wish to be at home, she and her children left in the carriage that would bring Mr Bennet back to Longbourn. She went away still as confused as ever about Elizabeth and her Derbyshire friend.

When Mr Bennet arrived, he had all the appearance of his usual calmness. He said as little as ever, and made no mention of the business that had taken him away, and it was some time before his daughters had the courage to speak of it.

It was not until the afternoon, when he joined them at tea, that Elizabeth dared to introduce the subject, and in answer to her expressions of sympathy, he said, 'Say nothing of that. It is right that I should suffer. It has been my own doing, and I ought to feel it.'

Then he continued, 'Lizzy, I have no bad feelings towards you for being right in your advice to me last May.'

They were interrupted by Jane, who came to collect her mother's tea.

'This is a ceremony,' he cried, 'which does me good! Another day I will behave as your mother does. I will sit in the library, and give as much trouble as I can – or perhaps I can delay it until Kitty runs away.'

'I am not going to run away, Father,' said Kitty. 'If I should ever go to Brighton, I would behave better than Lydia.'

'*You* go to Brighton! I will not trust you anywhere near it, not for fifty pounds! No, Kitty, I have at least learnt to be careful, and you will feel the effects of it. No officer is ever to enter this house again, or even to pass through the village. Balls are completely forbidden, unless you dance with one of your sisters. And you are never to go out of doors until you can prove that you have spent ten minutes of every day in a sensible manner.'

Kitty, who took all these threats seriously, began to cry.

'Well, well,' he said, 'do not make yourself unhappy. If you are a good girl for the next ten years, I will take you to the theatre at the end of them.'

Chapter 23   Lydia and Wickham Are Found

Two days after Mr Bennet's return, as Jane and Elizabeth were walking in the garden behind the house, they saw the housekeeper coming towards them.

'I beg your pardon, madam, for interrupting you,' she said to Jane, 'but I was hoping that you might have had good news from town, and I dared to come and ask.'

'What do you mean? We have heard nothing from town.'

'Dear madam,' cried the housekeeper, 'don't you know that an urgent letter came from Mr Gardiner half an hour ago?'

The girls ran away, too eager to reach the house to have time for speech. They ran through the hall into the breakfast room, and from there to the library. Their father was in neither. They were on the point of looking for him upstairs with their mother, when they were met by a manservant, who said:

'If you are looking for my master, madam, he is walking towards the little wood.'

They immediately left the house again, and ran across the grass after their father. Jane, who was not so light as Elizabeth, soon slowed down, while her sister, out of breath, reached him and eagerly cried out:

'Oh, Father, what news? Good or bad?'

'What good is to be expected?' he said, taking the letter from his pocket. 'But perhaps you would like to read it.'

Elizabeth impatiently caught it from his hand. Jane now came up and joined them.

'Read it out loud,' said their father.

Elizabeth read:

GRACECHURCH STREET
Monday, August 2nd

My dear brother,

At last I am able to send you some news. I have discovered my niece and the young man. They are not married, and I do not believe that they ever intended to be, but if you are willing to keep the promises that I have been forced to make in your name, I hope it will not be long before they are. All that is necessary is that you should settle on your daughter, by law, her equal share of the five thousand pounds that will come to your children after the death of yourself and my sister, and, in addition, that you should enter into an agreement to allow her, during your life, one hundred pounds a year. Mr Wickham's condition as regards money is not so hopeless as was believed, and I am happy to say that there will be a little of his own money left, even when his debts have been paid. There is not the smallest necessity for you to come to town, as I will give your lawyer all details about making the agreement. Send back your answer as soon as you can. We have judged it best that my niece should be married from this house, and I hope you will approve.

Yours, etc.

EDWARD GARDINER.

'And have you answered the letter?'

'I dislike it very much,' he replied, 'but it must be done.'

He turned back with them, and walked towards the house.

'And may I ask something?' said Elizabeth. 'The conditions must, I suppose, be agreed to?'

'Agreed to? I am only ashamed of his asking so little.'

'And they *must* marry! Even though he is *such* a man!'

'Yes, yes, there is nothing else to be done. But there are two things that I very much want to know – one is, how much money your uncle has paid out to arrange this, and the other, how I am ever going to pay him back.'

'Money! My uncle!' cried Jane. 'What do you mean, sir?'

'I mean that no man in his right mind would marry Lydia for so little as one hundred pounds a year.'

'That is very true,' said Elizabeth, 'though I had not thought of it before. His debts will be paid, and something will still remain! Oh, it must be my uncle's doing. Generous, good man! A small sum could not do all this.'

'No,' said her father, 'Wickham's a fool if he takes her with a penny less than ten thousand pounds.'

'Ten thousand pounds! How is half such a sum to be repaid?'

Mr Bennet made no answer, and each of them, deep in thought, continued to walk in silence until they reached the house. Their father then went to the library to write.

'And they are really to be married!' cried Elizabeth, as soon as she and Jane were by themselves. 'How strange this is! Although their chance of happiness is small, and his character is worthless, we are forced to be glad! Oh, Lydia!'

The girls now remembered that their mother probably knew nothing of what had happened. They went, therefore, and asked their father's permission to tell her. Without raising his head from his writing, he replied coldly:

'Just as you please.'

'May we take my uncle's letter to read to her?'

'Take whatever you like, and get away.'

After a slight warning of good news, the letter was read to Mrs Bennet. Their mother could hardly control herself. Her joy burst out after the first few sentences. She had no fears for her daughter's happiness, nor shame from any memory of her misbehaviour.

'This is so exciting!' she cried. 'She will be married at sixteen! How I wish to see her and dear Wickham too! But the clothes, the wedding clothes! I will write to my sister Gardiner about them directly. Ring the bell, Kitty, for the servant. I will dress in a moment. I will go to Meryton as soon as I am dressed, and tell the good, good news to my sister Philips. And as I am coming back, I can call on Lady Lucas and Mrs Long.'

She then began to tell the news to the servant, who expressed her joy. Elizabeth received her congratulations with the rest, and then, sick of this foolishness, went to her own room so that she could think in peace.

Chapter 24   Mr Bennet Agrees to Their Marriage

Mr Bennet had often wished, before this period in his life, that instead of spending his whole income, he had saved a yearly sum to provide for his children – and his wife, if she lived longer than he did. He now wished this more than ever. If he had done his duty in that matter, Lydia need not have depended on her uncle for whatever respectability could now be bought for her.

When Mr Bennet first married, saving was considered to be perfectly useless, for of course they would have a son. The son would, as heir, be willing at the age of twenty-one to make more suitable arrangements for the property, so that the wife and other children would be provided for. Five daughters, one after another, entered the world, but the son still did not come. They had, at last, given up hope, but it was then too late to begin saving. Mrs Bennet was naturally careless about money, and only her husband's love of independence prevented them from spending more than their income.

Five thousand pounds had been settled by marriage agreement on Mrs Bennet and her children, but the share that the children would receive depended on the wishes of the parents. This was one point, with regard to Lydia at least, which could now be settled, and Mr Bennet immediately accepted the proposal of his wife's brother. He had never supposed that the affair could have been arranged with so little inconvenience to himself. He would hardly be ten pounds poorer after hundred was paid each year to the young pair, because the cost of keeping Lydia at home – her pocket money, and the continual presents in money which passed to her through her mother's hands – amounted to very little less than that sum.

He wrote, therefore, to give his agreement and thanks to Mr Gardiner, but was too angry with Lydia to send any message to her.

It was two weeks since Mrs Bennet had last been downstairs, but on this happy day she again took her seat at the head of the table, and in extremely high spirits. No feeling of shame caused her joy to be lessened. Her thoughts ran completely on clothes, carriages, servants, and a large enough house for Lydia. Her husband allowed her to talk on without interruption while the servants remained. But when they had gone, he said to her, 'Mrs Bennet, before you take any or all of these houses for your daughter, understand that she shall never have admittance into this one, at least.'

A long argument followed this statement, but Mr Bennet was firm. It soon led to another, and Mrs Bennet found, with astonishment and shock, that her husband would not give one penny to buy clothes for her daughter. He declared that she should receive no sign of love whatever from him on the occasion. Mrs Bennet was more troubled by the shame of Lydia's lack of new clothes than the shame of the conditions which had made her marriage necessary.

Elizabeth was now deeply sorry that she had, in her unhappiness at the moment, made known to Mr Darcy her fears for her sister, since now Lydia's marriage would hide her earlier fault from all those who were not closely connected with the affair. She knew that she could trust him to keep the secret, but at the same time she was ashamed and full of sorrow that he, of all people, should know of her family's shame.

She felt sure that his wish to gain her respect would be destroyed by such a blow as this. She became desirous of his good opinion, when she could no longer hope to have the advantage of it. She wanted to hear of him, when there seemed the least chance of receiving information. She was quite sure now that she could have been happy with him, when it was no longer likely that they would meet.

What a victory for him, as she often thought, if he could only know that the proposals which she had so proudly scorned only four months ago would now have been gladly and gratefully received!

She began to realize that he was exactly the man who, in character and ability, would most suit her. It was a union that would have been to the advantage of both. By her confidence and liveliness, his mind might have been softened and his manners improved, and from his judgment, information and knowledge of the world, she would have received advantages of greater importance.

◆

The day of their sister's wedding arrived, and Jane and Elizabeth had urged their father so seriously but so gently to receive her and her husband at Longbourn after the event that he was at last persuaded to act as they wished. It would only be for a short time, as a move had been arranged for Wickham to another regiment stationed in the north of England, where he could make a fresh start in life.

The carriage was sent to meet them, and they were to return in it by dinnertime. Their arrival was expected by the two older Misses Bennet with a mixture of discomfort and anxiety.

They came. The family were waiting in the breakfast room to receive them. Smiles covered the face of Mrs Bennet as the carriage drove up to the door. Her husband looked serious, and her daughters anxious and nervous.

Lydia's voice was heard in the hall. The door was thrown open, and she ran into the room. Her mother stepped forward, kissed her, and welcomed her with joy, giving her hand with a warm smile to Wickham, who followed his lady.

Their welcome by Mr Bennet, to whom they then turned, was colder. His face became even more serious, and he hardly moved his lips. The easy confidence of the young pair was enough to anger him. Elizabeth was disgusted, and even Jane was shocked. Lydia was still Lydia, uncontrolled, unashamed, wild, noisy, fearless. She turned from one sister to another, demanding their congratulations, while Wickham was all smiles and easy politeness. Neither Lydia nor her mother could talk fast enough.

'To think that it has been three months,' cried Lydia, 'since I went away! I am sure that I had no idea of being married before I came back, though I thought it would be very good fun if I was.'

Her father lifted his eyes, and Elizabeth looked expressively at her, but she continued brightly, 'Oh, mother, do the people at Meryton know I am married today? I was afraid they might not, so as we came through I let my hand rest on the window frame of the carriage, so that they could see the ring.'

As they passed through the hall to the dining room, Lydia, with anxious importance, walked up to her mother's right hand, and said to her oldest sister, 'Ah, Jane, I take your place now, and you must go lower, because I am a married woman.'

'Well, mother,' she said, after the meal, 'what do you think of my husband? Is he not a fine-looking man? I am sure that my sisters must all be jealous of me. I only hope that they may have half my good luck. They must all go to Brighton. That is the place to get husbands. Or you must all come and see us in the north. I expect that there will be some dances, and I will take care to get good partners for my sisters. And then, when you go away, you may leave one or two of them behind, and I am sure that I shall get husbands for them before the winter is over.'

'I thank you for your advice,' said Elizabeth, 'but I do not especially like your way of getting husbands.'

Wickham's love for Lydia was just what Elizabeth had expected it to be – not equal to Lydia's for him. She guessed that their running away together had been caused by the strength of *her* love rather than by his, and that escape from his debts had been the main reason for his leaving Brighton, though he was not the kind of young man to refuse the opportunity of having a companion.

Lydia was extremely fond of him. He was her dear Wickham on every occasion. No one could be compared with him. He did everything best in the world.

One morning soon after their arrival, as she was sitting with her two oldest sisters, she said to Elizabeth:

'Lizzy, I never gave you an account of my wedding. You were not present when I told the others. Are you not interested in hearing how it was managed?'

'No, really,' replied Elizabeth, 'I think there cannot be too little said on the subject.'

'Oh! How strange you are! But I must tell you how it happened. Well, the day came, and I was so excited! I was so afraid, you know, that something would happen to delay it. And there was my aunt, all the time that I was dressing, talking away just as if she were a minister in church. But I did not hear a word of it, because I was thinking about whether my dear Wickham would be married in his blue coat. Well, and just as the carriage came to the door, my uncle was called away on business. I was so frightened that I did not know what to do, because my uncle was to act in place of my father at the ceremony, and give me in marriage, and if we were late we could not be married all day. But I remembered afterwards that it need not have been delayed, because Mr Darcy might have taken his place.'

'Mr Darcy!' repeated Elizabeth in astonishment.

'Oh, yes! He came there with Wickham, you know. But heavens! I quite forgot! I promised not to mention it. It was a secret.'

'In that case,' said Elizabeth, although she was burning with a desire to know more, 'we will ask you no questions.'

'Thank you,' said Lydia, 'because if you did, I should certainly tell you all, and then Wickham would be so angry.'

With such encouragement, Elizabeth was forced to help her sister keep her secret by leaving the room.

But it was impossible not to ask for information on this matter. Mr Darcy had been at her sister's wedding! What could be the reason? Seizing a sheet of paper, she wrote a short letter to her aunt to request an explanation, if it could be given without breaking confidence. 'And if it cannot,' she added at the end of the letter, 'and if you do not tell me in an honourable manner, my dear aunt, I shall certainly be forced to use some trick to find out!'

♦

Elizabeth had the satisfaction of receiving an immediate answer to her letter. As soon as she was in possession of it, she hurried off to the little wood, where she was least likely to be interrupted.

GRACECHURCH STREET
September 6th

My dear niece,

I have just received your letter and must admit to being surprised by your request. Don't think me angry, though, because I only mean that I had not imagined such inquiries to be necessary on *your* side. Your uncle is as much surprised as I am, and nothing but the belief of your involvement in the affair would have allowed him to act as he has done. But if you really know nothing of the matter, I must give you an explanation.

On the same day as my return from Longbourn, your uncle had a most unexpected visit from Mr Darcy, who talked with him in private for several hours. He came to tell Mr Gardiner that he had found out where your sister and Mr Wickham were, and that he had talked to them. From what I can understand, he left Derbyshire only one day after ourselves, and came to town with the intention of hunting for them. He generously gave as a reason for this that he felt himself responsible for the whole situation, because he had not made public in Meryton last year his knowledge of Wickham's worthlessness. He blamed his own pride for this.

It seems that there is a lady who was formerly a private teacher to Miss Darcy and who was dismissed for some good reason that he did not mention. She had then rented a house in London and supported herself by letting rooms. Knowing that she had been friendly with Mr Wickham, Darcy went to her, and succeeded with some difficulty in getting his address. He first tried to persuade Lydia to leave her shameful situation and return to her friends, but he found her determined to remain where she was. She was sure that Wickham would marry her sometime or other, and it did not much matter when. The gentleman himself, it appeared, had no such intention. He still hoped to make his fortune by a good marriage in some other place. But an agreement was at last reached which was satisfactory to both sides.

Our visitor, Darcy, refused every attempt by Mr Gardiner to share these responsibilities. Nothing was done that he did not do himself, though I am sure that your uncle would most willingly have settled the whole matter. They argued over it together for a long time, but at last your uncle was forced to agree. Wickham's debts will be paid, another thousand pounds will be settled on her, and a good position in the army will be obtained for him.

There may be some truth in the reasons given by Mr Darcy for acting so generously, but in spite of all this fine talk, my dear Lizzy, you may be sure that your uncle would never have agreed if we had not believed him to have *another interest* in the affair. Will you be very angry if I take this opportunity of saying how much I like him? His behaviour, his understanding and opinions all please me, and he only lacks a little liveliness, and *that*, if he marries the *right* person, his wife may teach him. I thought him very secretive. He hardly ever mentioned your name. But secrecy seems to be the fashion. Please forgive me if I have said too much, or at least do not punish me so far as to forbid me to visit you at P.

But I must write no more. The children have been wanting me for the last half-hour.

Your loving aunt,

M. GARDINER.

The information in this letter unsettled Elizabeth's spirits. Darcy had done all this for a woman whom he must scorn and the man whom he most wished to avoid! Her heart *did* whisper that he had done it for *her*. Oh, how sorry she was for every unkind feeling that she had ever encouraged towards him! For herself, she felt ashamed and small, but she was proud of him – proud that in a cause of honour he could defeat his own nature. She read over her aunt's praise of him again and again. It was hardly enough, but it pleased her.

Chapter 25   Return to Netherfield

The day soon arrived when the young pair had to leave, and Mrs Bennet was forced to bear the separation.

'Write to me often, my dear Lydia,' she cried.

'As often as I can, but married women never have much time for writing. My sisters may write to *me*. They will have nothing else to do.'

Mr Wickham's goodbyes were much warmer than his wife's. He smiled a lot and said many pretty things.

As soon as he was out of the house, Mr Bennet said bitterly: 'He is as fine a young man as ever I saw. He smiles sweetly, and makes love to us all. I am extremely proud of him. Even Sir William Lucas could not produce a better husband for his daughter.'

The loss of Lydia made Mrs Bennet very dull for several days, but her spiritless condition was relieved soon afterwards by a piece of news which then began to be passed round. The housekeeper at Netherfield had received orders to prepare for the arrival of her master. Mrs Bennet was quite unsettled. She looked at Jane, and smiled and shook her head.

Jane had not been able to hear of his arrival without trembling a little, and Elizabeth could easily see that it had had an effect on her spirits. Elizabeth herself was confused by the visit. Had he come with his friend's permission, or was he brave enough to act without it?

'I am beginning to be sorry that he is coming at all,' said Jane to Elizabeth a few days later. 'It would be nothing, I could see him with complete lack of interest, but I can hardly bear to hear it continually talked about. My mother means well, but she does not know how I suffer from what she says.'

Mr Bingley arrived. On the third morning after his coming, Mrs Bennet saw him from her dressing-room window as he rode towards the house.

Her daughters were eagerly called on to share her joy. Jane firmly stayed at her place at the table, but Elizabeth, to satisfy her mother, went to the window.

She looked, saw Mr Darcy with him, and sat down again by her sister.

'There is a gentleman with Mr Bingley, Mama,' said Kitty. 'It looks like that tall, proud man, who used to be with him before – I've forgotten his name.'

'Oh, heavens! Mr Darcy! Well, I must say that I hate the sight of him.'

Both Elizabeth and Jane were uncomfortable, but the former

had a cause for discomfort which could not be guessed by Jane, to whom she had never yet had the courage to show Mrs Gardiner's letter, or to tell of her own change of feeling. Her astonishment at his coming and wishing to see her again was almost as great as she had experienced when she had first observed his changed behaviour in Derbyshire. Her face, which had become pale for half a minute, now found its colour again with an additional warmth, and a smile of pleasure added brightness to her eyes, as she thought that his love and wishes must still be unchanged – but she could not be sure.

She sat busily at work, trying not to appear excited. Jane looked a little paler than usual. When the gentlemen appeared, she received them fairly calmly. Elizabeth said as little as politeness would allow, and sat again at her work. She had dared to take only one look at Darcy. He looked serious as usual.

Bingley, she saw, was both pleased and confused. He was received by Mrs Bennet with an amount of attention which made her two oldest daughters feel ashamed, especially when it was compared with the cold and ceremonious politeness of her behaviour to his friend. Elizabeth especially, who knew what her mother owed to Mr Darcy.

Darcy said hardly anything to her. He was not seated by her, so perhaps that was the reason for his silence. When sometimes, unable to prevent it, she raised her eyes to his face, she found him looking at Jane quite as often as at herself. She was disappointed, and angry with herself for being so.

At this time Mrs Bennet was talking to Bingley happily about Lydia's marriage, and receiving his congratulations.

'It is a satisfying thing, to be sure, to have a daughter married,' Mrs Bennet continued, 'but at the same time it is very hard to have her taken away from me. Her husband has been moved to another regiment, you know. Thank heavens he has *some* friends, though not, perhaps, as many as he deserves.'

Elizabeth, who knew that this was directed against Mr Darcy, thought that she could now feel no greater shame. But her discomfort soon received relief from seeing how much the beauty of her sister was bringing back the admiration of her former lover, who seemed to be giving her more and more of his attention.

When the gentlemen rose to go, they were invited to eat at Longbourn in a few days' time.

◆

As soon as they had gone, Elizabeth walked in the garden to recover her spirits. Mr Darcy's behaviour astonished and confused her. She could explain it in no way that gave her pleasure.

'Why did he come at all, if it was only to be silent and serious? If he fears me, why come here? If he no longer cares for me, why be silent? Annoying man! I will think no more about him.'

Her sister approached, and joined her with a cheerful smile.

'Now,' she said, 'that this first meeting is over, I feel perfectly relaxed. I am glad that he will eat here on Tuesday. It will then be publicly seen that we meet only as ordinary and uninterested acquaintances.'

'Very uninterested!' said Elizabeth laughingly. 'I think that you are in very great danger of making him as much in love with you as ever.'

They did not see the gentlemen again until Tuesday, when there was a large party at Longbourn. As the two men entered the dining room, Elizabeth eagerly watched to see whether Bingley would take the place which, at all their former parties, had belonged to him, by her sister. Her careful mother, having the same idea, did not invite him to sit by herself. He seemed to pause, but Jane looked round and smiled. It was decided. He placed himself beside her.

Elizabeth, with a feeling of victory, looked towards his friend. He bore it well, and she would have imagined that Bingley had received his permission to be happy, if she had not seen his eyes turned towards Mr Darcy with an expression of anxiety.

His behaviour towards her sister during dinner showed such admiration that Elizabeth believed that, if left completely to himself, Jane's happiness, and his own, would be speedily gained.

Mr Darcy was on one side of her mother. She knew how little such a situation could give pleasure to either. She was not near enough to hear any of their conversation, but she could see how rarely they spoke to each other, and how formal and cold their manner was whenever they did.

She hoped that the evening would provide some opportunity of bringing herself and Mr Darcy together. Anxious and uncomfortable, the period which passed in the sitting room before the gentlemen came in was tiring and dull.

The gentlemen came, and she thought that he looked as if he would have answered her hopes, but oh! the ladies had crowded so closely round the table, where Jane was making tea and Elizabeth pouring out the coffee, that there was not a single space near her where a chair could be placed. He walked away to another part of the room.

She was a little cheered, though, by his bringing back his coffee cup himself, and she seized the opportunity to inquire after his sister. He replied, and then stood beside her for some minutes in silence.

When the tea things had been removed, and the card tables placed, they were seated far from each other, at different games, and she lost every expectation of pleasure. Mrs Bennet was in high spirits when the guests had gone.

'Well, girls,' she said, as soon as they were left to themselves, 'I think everything passed off uncommonly well. The dinner was as well cooked as any I ever saw. The meat was cooked to perfection. The soup was 50 times better than that we had at the Lucases' last week. And, my dear Jane, what do you think Mrs Long said? "Ah, Mrs Bennet, we shall have her at Netherfield at last!" I do think that Mrs Long is as good a woman as ever lived – and her nieces are very well-behaved girls, and not at all good-looking. I like them very much.'

♦

A few days later, Mr Bingley called again, and alone. His friend had left that morning for London, but would return in ten days' time. He sat with them for over an hour, and was in noticeably good spirits. Mrs Bennet invited him to dinner with them, but unfortunately he had another engagement. He eagerly accepted an invitation, though, for the following day.

He came, and so early that none of the ladies was dressed. Mrs Bennet ran into her daughter's room with her hair half-finished, crying out:

'My dear Jane, hurry down. He has come. Hurry, hurry.'

'We shall be down as soon as we can,' said Jane, 'but I dare say that Kitty will be ready before either of us.'

'Oh, never mind about Kitty! What has she to do with it? Come, be quick!'

The same anxiety to get Jane and Mr Bingley by themselves was plain again in the evening. After tea, Mr Bennet went to the library, as was his custom, and Mary went upstairs to her piano. Two of the five being removed, Mrs Bennet sat making signals with her eyes at Elizabeth and Kitty for some time, without having any effect on them. Elizabeth did not take any notice, and when at last Kitty did, she said in surprise, 'What is the matter, Mother? Is something wrong? What should I do?'

'Nothing, child, nothing.'

Five minutes later, she suddenly got up, and saying to Kitty, 'Come here, my love, I want to speak to you,' took her out of the room. A look from Jane begged Elizabeth to remain, but when, some moments later, the door half opened and her mother called out that she wanted her, she was forced to go.

Her mother announced her intention of sitting upstairs, and as soon as she was out of sight, Elizabeth returned to the sitting room.

Bingley was everything a gentleman should be for the rest of the evening. He bore all Mrs Bennet's silly remarks with the greatest patience. After this day, Jane said no more about being uninterested. Elizabeth believed that all must speedily be brought to a successful ending, unless Mr Darcy returned too soon. She felt, though, that all this must be happening with that gentleman's approval.

Bingley spent the next morning shooting with Mr Bennet, and returned with him to dinner. After the meal Elizabeth had a letter to write and, believing that the others were all going to sit down together to cards, she went to her own room.

But on returning to the sitting room, she found that her mother had again been arranging matters. Her sister and Bingley were standing together by the fireplace as if in serious conversation, and the faces of both, as they quickly turned and moved away from each other, told everything. Not a word was said by either, and Elizabeth in her confusion was just going away again, when Bingley suddenly whispered a few words to her sister, and ran out of the room.

Jane could have no secrets from Elizabeth, and immediately admitted that she was the happiest being in the world. Elizabeth's congratulations were given with sincerity and pleasure. Jane then ran to her mother.

In a few minutes Elizabeth was joined by Mr Bingley, whose conversation with Mr Bennet had been short and successful. He claimed her good wishes and love as a sister, and they shook hands with great pleasure.

It was an evening of excitement for them all. Jane's happiness made her look more beautiful than ever. Kitty smiled, and hoped that her turn was coming soon. Mrs Bennet could not express her feelings often enough, and when Mr Bennet joined them at supper, his voice and manner plainly showed how happy he was.

Not a word passed his lips about it until his visitor had gone. He then turned to his daughter and said:

'Jane, I congratulate you. You will be a very happy woman.'

Jane went to him, kissed him, and thanked him for his goodness.

'You are a good girl,' he replied, 'and I have no doubt that you will suit each other. You are each so ready to give way to the other that nothing will ever be decided on; so trusting that every servant will cheat you, and so generous that you will always spend more than your income.'

'Spend more than their income!' cried his wife. 'My dear Mr Bennet, what are you talking of? He has four or five thousand pounds a year, and very likely more.' Then, addressing her daughter, 'Oh, my dear, dear Jane, I am so happy! I am sure that I shall not get a moment's sleep tonight. I knew that you could not be so beautiful for nothing. Oh, he is the best-looking young man that ever was seen!'

Wickham, Lydia, were all forgotten. Jane was at that moment her favourite child, and she cared for no other.

Bingley, from this time, was of course a daily visitor at Longbourn. The situation could not remain a secret for long. Mrs Bennet whispered it to Mrs Philips, who passed on the news without permission to all her neighbours. The Bennets were spoken of as the luckiest family in the world, though only a few weeks before, when Lydia had run away, they had been generally believed to be the most unfortunate.

Chapter 26   Lady Catherine Visits Longbourn

One morning, about a week later, a carriage suddenly appeared outside the house. It was too early for visitors, and neither the carriage nor the uniform of the servant was familiar. The two lovers immediately escaped to the garden, leaving the rest of the ladies to guess who the stranger could be, until the door was thrown open and Lady Catherine de Bourgh entered.

She walked in, looking more disagreeable than usual, made no other reply to Elizabeth's greeting than a slight movement of the head, and sat down without a word.

After sitting for a moment in silence, she said, very stiffly, to Elizabeth:

'I hope you are well, Miss Bennet. That lady, I suppose, is your mother?'

Elizabeth replied shortly that she was.

'And *that*, I suppose, is one of your sisters?'

'Yes, madam,' replied Mrs Bennet, to whom Elizabeth had mentioned the visitor's name, and who was feeling highly honoured by her coming.

'You have a very small park here,' observed Lady Catherine, after a short silence, 'and this must be a most inconvenient sitting room for the evening in summer. The windows appear to be facing west.'

Mrs Bennet informed her that they never sat there after dinner, and then added:

'May I ask whether you left Mr and Mrs Collins well?'

'Yes, very well.'

Elizabeth now expected that she would produce a letter for her from Charlotte, because it seemed the only likely reason for her visit. But no letter appeared, and she could not understand the visit at all.

Mrs Bennet, with great politeness, begged Lady Catherine to

have something to eat or drink, but this was decidedly, and not very politely, refused. Then, rising, Lady Catherine said to Elizabeth: 'Miss Bennet, I should be glad to take a walk in your garden, if you will give me your company.'

Elizabeth obeyed. As they passed through the hall, Lady Catherine opened the doors of the other rooms, and announced that they were a reasonably good size.

They walked in silence towards the little wood. Elizabeth was determined to make no effort at conversation with a woman who was now more than usually rude and disagreeable.

As soon as they entered the wood, Lady Catherine began in the following manner:

'You can have no difficulty, Miss Bennet, in understanding the reason of my visit. Your own heart, your own conscience must tell you why I have come.'

Elizabeth looked at her in astonishment.

'Miss Bennet,' she continued in an angry voice, 'you ought to know that I will not be treated without proper regard for my position. A report of a most upsetting nature reached me two days ago. I was told that you, Miss Elizabeth Bennet, would in all probability be soon united to my nephew, my own nephew. Though I *know* that it must be a shameful lie, I immediately decided to come here so that I could make my feelings known to you.'

'If you believed it impossible,' said Elizabeth, her face turning red with astonishment and scorn, 'I am surprised that you took the trouble of coming so far.'

'This is not to be borne. Miss Bennet, I will be satisfied. Has he, has my nephew, made you an offer of marriage?'

'You have said that it is impossible.'

'Miss Bennet, do you know who I am? Let me be rightly understood. Mr Darcy is engaged to my daughter. Now, what have you to say?'

'Only this – that if it is so, you can have no reason to suppose that he will make an offer to me.'

Lady Catherine paused for a moment, and then replied:

'The arrangement between them is of a special kind. From their childhood they have been intended for each other. It was the favourite wish of his mother, as well as of myself. Have you no respect for the wishes of his relations?'

'But what is that to me? If Mr Darcy wishes, may he not make another choice? And if I am that choice, why may I not accept him?'

'I will not be interrupted! Hear me in silence. I see there is a seat over there. Let us sit down. My daughter and my nephew are made for each other. Their birth and their fortunes are noble. And what will divide them? The plans of a young woman without rank or money?'

'Your nephew is a gentleman, and I am a gentleman's daughter.'

'But what is your mother? Who are your uncles and aunts? Do you imagine that I am without knowledge of their condition?'

'If your nephew does not object to them,' replied Elizabeth, 'it can be nothing to you.'

'Tell me, are you engaged to him?'

Elizabeth could only say: 'I am not.' Lady Catherine seemed pleased.

'And will you promise never to become engaged to my nephew?'

'I will make no promise of any kind.'

'Miss Bennet, I am shocked. The facts concerning your youngest sister are fully known to me. Is such a girl to be my nephew's sister? Is *her* husband, the son of his father's servant, to be his brother?'

'You can now have nothing further to say to me,' Elizabeth

116

answered with bitterness. 'You have insulted me in every possible way. I must beg to return to the house.'

She rose as she spoke. Lady Catherine also rose, highly angered. She talked on, making many threats, until they were at the door of her carriage, when, suddenly turning round, she added:

'I leave you without a goodbye, Miss Bennet. I send no greetings to your mother. You do not deserve such attention. I am most seriously displeased.'

Elizabeth made no answer, but walked quietly into the house. Her mother met her impatiently. 'Had she anything special to say, Lizzy?'

Elizabeth was forced to tell a small lie here, for to admit the truth about their conversation was impossible.

◆

This astonishing visit upset Elizabeth for some time. She could not imagine what could be the origin of the report that she was engaged, unless talk had followed the news about Jane and Bingley. She could not help feeling some discomfort about the result of Lady Catherine's words, because she did not know the degree of her influence over her nephew. If he had been holding back before, his aunt's arguments might settle every doubt.

'If, therefore, an excuse for not returning should come to his friend within a few days,' she thought, 'I shall lose all hope in the strength of his love.'

The next morning, as she was going downstairs, she was met by her father, who came out of his library with a letter in his hand.

'Lizzy,' he said, 'I was going to look for you. Come into my room.'

She followed him in, and they both sat down. He then said:

'I have received a letter this morning concerning yourself that astonishes me. I did not know that I had *two* daughters about to be married. Let me congratulate you.'

She now reddened in the immediate belief that it was a letter from the nephew instead of the aunt. He continued:

'You look self-conscious, but I am sure that you cannot guess the name of your admirer. This letter is from Mr Collins.'

'From Mr Collins! And what can he have to say?'

'He begins with congratulations about Jane. He then goes on: "Your daughter Elizabeth, it is supposed, will also not long bear the name of Bennet, and her future partner has every kind of good fortune, in property, relations and influence. Yet in spite of all these, let me warn my cousin Elizabeth and yourself of the risks that she runs in accepting this gentleman's proposals." Have you any idea, Lizzy, who this gentleman is? But now it comes out. "His aunt, Lady Catherine de Bourgh, does not look on the relationship with a friendly eye." *Mr Darcy*, you see, is the man! Now, Lizzy, I think that I *have* surprised you! Could he have chosen a more unlikely man? Mr Darcy, who probably never looked at you in his life!'

Elizabeth tried to join in her father's amusement, but could only force one unwilling smile. His joking had never been so little pleasing to her.

'Are you not amused?'

'Oh, yes! Please read on.'

'He continues: "I thought it my duty to give information of this immediately to my cousin, so that she and her noble admirer may not act without careful thought." After that he adds, "I am truly happy that my cousin Lydia's sad business has been so well hidden. But I must not neglect the duties of my position, and must state my astonishment on hearing that you received the young pair into your house. You ought certainly to forgive them, but never to admit them to your sight or allow their names to be mentioned." *That* is his idea of forgiveness! But Lizzy, you look as if you did not enjoy it. You are not going to pretend to be insulted, I hope, by stupid talk. For what do we live, if not to amuse our neighbours, and laugh at them in our turn?'

'I am extremely amused!' said Elizabeth. 'But it is so strange!'

'Yes, if they had fixed on any other man, it would have been nothing. But *his* complete lack of interest in you, and *your* sharp dislike of him, make it so particularly entertaining! And Lizzy, what did Lady Catherine say about this report? Did she call to refuse her agreement?'

To this question his daughter replied only with a laugh, and as it had been asked without the least suspicion, she was not put into an awkward position by his repeating it. Elizabeth had never found it more difficult to make her feelings appear what they were not. It was necessary to laugh, when she would rather have cried. Her father had most cruelly wounded her by what he said of Mr Darcy's lack of interest, and she feared that perhaps instead of his noticing too *little*, she might have imagined too *much*.

Chapter 27　Elizabeth and Mr Darcy

Instead of receiving any such letter of excuse from his friend, as Elizabeth half expected Mr Bingley to do, he was able to bring Darcy with him to Longbourn before many days had passed. The gentlemen arrived early, and Bingley suggested that they all go for a walk. Mrs Bennet was not in the habit of walking, and Mary could never give up the time, but the remaining five set out together. Bingley and Jane, though, soon allowed the others to get ahead of them, and Elizabeth, Kitty and Darcy were left to entertain each other.

Kitty wanted to call on the Lucases, and when she left the other two, Elizabeth went on bravely with Darcy alone. She had secretly been making a difficult decision, and perhaps he had been doing the same. Now was the moment to put hers into action, so she said:

'Mr Darcy, I am a very selfish creature, and, in order to give relief to my own feelings, do not care how much I may be wounding yours. I can no longer help thanking you for your deep kindness to my poor sister.'

'I am sorry,' replied Darcy, in a voice full of surprise and feeling, 'that you have ever been informed of what may, by mistake, have given you discomfort of mind.'

'Do not blame my aunt. Lydia's thoughtlessness first caused the truth to be known, and I could not rest until I knew the details. Let me thank you again, in the name of all my family.'

'If you *will* thank me,' he replied, 'let it be for yourself alone. Your family owe me nothing. Much as I respect them, I believe that I thought only of you.'

Elizabeth was too confused to say a word. After a short pause, her companion added: 'You are too generous to keep me in uncertainty. If your feelings are still what they were last April, tell me so at once. My love and wishes are unchanged, but one word from you will silence me on this subject for ever.'

Elizabeth now forced herself to speak, and made him understand that her feelings had changed so completely since that period that she was grateful and pleased to hear his present words. The happiness that this reply produced was greater than he had probably ever experienced before, and he expressed himself on the occasion as warmly as a man who is violently in love can be expected to do.

They walked on without knowing in what direction. There was too much to be thought, and felt, and said, for attention to anything else. She soon learnt that they owed their present good understanding to the efforts of his aunt, who *did* call on him to describe her conversation with Elizabeth, but with the opposite effect to that which she intended.

'It taught me to hope,' he said, 'as I had hardly allowed myself to hope before. I knew enough of your character to be certain that if you had been completely decided against me, you would have admitted it to Lady Catherine openly.'

Elizabeth laughed as she replied, 'Yes, you knew enough of my readiness to speak plainly to believe that I was able to do that. After criticizing you so shamefully to your face, I could have no fear of criticizing you to your relations.'

'What did you say of me that I did not deserve? For though your charges were mistaken, my behaviour to you then was unpardonable. I have been selfish all my life. Unfortunately, I was spoiled by my parents, who, though good themselves, encouraged me to be proud and to think with scorn of the rest of the world. That is how I was, and how I might still be if I had not met you, dearest Elizabeth! You taught me a lesson, a hard one, but most advantageous. You showed me how small were all my claims to please a woman who deserved to be pleased.'

'I am almost afraid to ask what you thought of me when we met at Pemberley. Did you blame me for coming?'

'No, no, I felt nothing but surprise.'

'I admit that I did not expect to be so well received.'

'My aim then,' replied Darcy, 'was to show you, by every attention, that I had no bad feelings for you, and I hoped to obtain your forgiveness, and lessen your bad opinion of me, by letting you see that I was trying to cure my faults.'

After walking several miles in an unhurried manner, they examined their watches and found that it was time to be at home.

Wherever were Mr Bingley and Jane! This thought introduced a discussion of their affairs. Darcy was very happy that they had become engaged.

'I must ask you whether you were surprised,' said Elizabeth.

'Not at all. When I went away, I felt it would happen.'

121

'That is to say, you had given your permission.' And though he refused to say so, she found that it was very much the case.

'I told him, before I left, that I thought that I had given him mistaken advice, and that I had been at fault in supposing your sister did not care for him.'

'Did you speak from what you had seen yourself, or only from my information last spring?'

'From the former. I watched your sister closely during the two visits which I recently made here, and I felt sure of her love for Bingley.'

Elizabeth would have liked to remark that Mr Bingley was a most satisfactory friend, so easily guided, but she controlled herself. She remembered that Darcy still had to learn to be laughed at, and it was rather early to begin.

They continued in conversation until they reached the house, and parted in the hall.

◆

'My dear Lizzy, where have you been walking to?' was the question which Elizabeth received from Jane as soon as she entered the room, and from all the others when they sat down to table. She had only to say that they had wandered about until they had lost their way. Her face turned slightly red as she spoke, but nobody suspected the truth.

The evening passed quietly. It was not in Darcy's nature to express happiness through high spirits, and Elizabeth was thinking of what her family would feel when everything was known.

At night, she opened her heart to Jane.

'You are joking, Lizzy. Engaged to Mr Darcy! No, no, you shall not deceive me. I know that it is impossible.'

'But, it's true, I am serious. I speak nothing but the truth.'

'Oh, Lizzy, I know how much you dislike him.'

'*That* is all forgotten. Perhaps I did not always love him as well as I do now.'

'But are you certain – forgive the question – are you quite certain that you can be happy with him?'

'There can be no doubt of that. But are you pleased, Jane?'

'Very, very much. Nothing could give Bingley or myself greater pleasure. Oh, Lizzy, are you sure that you feel what you ought to feel?'

'I am only afraid you will think that I feel *more* than I ought, when I tell you all.'

'What do you mean?'

'Well, I must admit that I love him better than I do Bingley. I am afraid that you will be angry.'

'My dearest sister, be serious. Will you tell me how long you have loved him?'

'I believe that I must date it from my first seeing his beautiful grounds at Pemberley.'

Another request that she should be serious produced the desired effect, and she soon made Jane believe in her sincerity. Elizabeth told the reasons for her former secrecy: her unsettled feelings, and her unwillingness to mention Bingley, which she could hardly have avoided doing if she had spoken of the meeting in Derbyshire. Half the night was spent in conversation.

'Oh, heavens!' cried Mrs Bennet, as she stood at the window the next morning. 'That disagreeable Mr Darcy is coming here again with our dear Bingley! What can he mean by being so annoying? Lizzy, you must walk out with him again, so that he will not be in Bingley's way.'

Elizabeth could hardly help laughing at so convenient a proposal, but she was really annoyed that her mother should be speaking of him in such a manner.

As soon as they entered, Bingley looked at her so expressively, and shook hands with such warmth, that she was in no doubt of his knowledge, and he soon afterwards said, 'Mrs Bennet, have you no more country roads round about here, in which Lizzy may lose her way again today?'

'I advise Mr Darcy and Lizzy and Kitty,' said Mrs Bennet, 'to walk to Oakham Mount this morning. It is a nice long walk, and Mr Darcy has never seen the view.'

'I am sure that it would be too much for Kitty,' said Bingley.

Kitty admitted that she would rather stay at home. As Elizabeth went upstairs, her mother followed her, saying:

'I am sorry, Lizzy, that you should be forced to have that disagreeable man all to yourself, but it is all for Jane, you know. There is no need to talk to him, except just now and then, so do not put yourself to inconvenience.'

During the walk, it was decided that Mr Bennet's agreement to the marriage should be asked during the evening. Elizabeth kept for herself the duty of asking her mother's.

In the evening, soon after Mr Bennet had gone to his library, Mr Darcy followed him. Elizabeth's anxiety was extreme. She did not fear her father's opposition, but that *she* should be making him unhappy by her choice was a troubling thought. She was a little relieved by Darcy's smile on his return, when he whispered to her, 'Go to your father.' She went directly.

Her father was walking about the room, looking serious. 'Lizzy,' he said, 'what are you doing? Are you out of your mind, to be accepting this man? Have you not always hated him?'

How deeply she then wished that her former opinions had been more reasonable, and her expression of them less extreme! It would have saved her explanations that it was very awkward to give. She told him, in some confusion, of the strength of her feelings for Mr Darcy.

'That is to say, you are determined to have him. He is rich, to be sure, and you may have more fine clothes and fine carriages than Jane. But will they make you happy? We all know him to be a proud, unpleasant man.'

'I do, I do like him,' she replied, with tears in her eyes. 'And what you say of him is untrue. You do not know what he really is.'

'Lizzy,' said her father, 'I have agreed. But let me advise you to think better of it. I know your nature, Lizzy. I know that you could not be happy unless you truly respected your husband. My child, do not let me have the unhappiness of seeing you unable to think well of your partner in life.'

At last, by repeating that Mr Darcy was really the object of her choice, by explaining the gradual change in her feelings, and her proof of the unchanging nature of his, and describing with energy all his good qualities, she did persuade her father to believe her, and make him satisfied with her choice. To complete his favourable opinion, she then told him what Mr Darcy had done for Lydia.

'Well, my dear,' he said, when she had finished speaking, 'if this is the case, he deserves you. I could not have parted with you, my Lizzy, to anyone who did not.'

He then reminded her of her confusion a few days before when he was reading Mr Collins's letter and, after laughing at her, allowed her to go, saying as she left the room, 'If any young men come for Mary or Kitty, send them in. I am not busy.'

Elizabeth's mind was now relieved of a very heavy weight, and after half an hour's quiet thought in her own room, she was able to join the others in fairly settled spirits.

When her mother went up to her dressing room at night, she followed her and made the important announcement. Its effect was most astonishing. When she heard it, Mrs Bennet sat quite still, unable to say a word. Only after many, many minutes could she understand what she had heard. She began at last to recover, to move about in her chair, get up, sit down again, and every now and then let out a small laugh.

'Oh, heavens! Lord save me! Only think! Mr Darcy! Who would have thought it! Oh, my sweetest Lizzy, how rich and great you will be! What jewels, what carriages you will have! Jane's is nothing to it – nothing at all. Such a pleasant man! So good-looking! So tall! Oh, my dear Lizzy! Do apologize for my having disliked him so much before. Dear, dear Lizzy. A house in town! Three daughters married! Ten thousand a year! Oh, heavens! What will happen to me? I shall go out of my mind.'

This was an unpleasing example of what her mother's behaviour might be like in the presence of Mr Darcy, but the next day passed off better than Elizabeth expected. Luckily Mrs Bennet was so filled with respect for her intended son-in-law that she did not dare to speak to him, except to offer him some mark of attention.

Elizabeth had the satisfaction of seeing her father making every effort to know him better, and Mr Bennet soon informed her that Mr Darcy was rising in his opinion every hour.

Chapter 28   The End

It was a happy day for all her feelings as a mother, when Mrs Bennet saw her two most deserving daughters married. It may be guessed that she afterwards visited Mrs Bingley, and talked of Mrs Darcy, with excited pride. I wish I could say that the satisfaction of her dreams for them made her a sensible woman for the rest of her life, though perhaps it was lucky for her husband's amusement that she still often had an attack of nerves, and was never anything but silly.

Mr Bennet missed his second daughter very much. His love for her caused him to travel from home more often than anything else could do. He enjoyed going to Pemberley, especially when he was least expected.

Mr Bingley and Jane remained at Netherfield for only a year. The nearness of her mother was not desirable even to his kindly nature or her loving heart. He then bought a property in Derbyshire, and Jane and Elizabeth, in addition to every other happiness, lived within 30 miles of each other.

Kitty, to her very great advantage, spent most of her time with her two older sisters. In society that was so much better than what she had generally known, her improvement was great. She was not of so uncontrollable a nature as Lydia, and when she was removed from the influence of her example became less complaining and less silly. Although Lydia frequently invited her to come and stay with her, with promises of dances and young men, her father would never allow her to go.

Mary was the only daughter who remained at home, and she was necessarily interrupted in her studies and her efforts at making music by the fact that Mrs Bennet was quite unable to sit alone. Mary was forced to mix more with the world, and as her more beautiful sisters were no longer there to be compared with her, she was not unwilling to do so.

As for Lydia and Wickham, their characters remained unchanged. He bore with calmness the knowledge that Elizabeth must now have learnt every detail about his past, and both he and Lydia were not without hope that Darcy could still be persuaded to make his fortune. Elizabeth did frequently send some relief from her own private money, and because of his love for Elizabeth, Darcy helped Wickham to get a better position in the army. Although her husband could never be received at Pemberley, Lydia was sometimes a visitor there, and they both of them frequently stayed so long with the Bingleys that even Bingley's good temper failed him.

Miss Bingley was much annoyed by Darcy's marriage, but as she wanted to continue to visit Pemberley, she was forced to be polite to Elizabeth.

Pemberley was now Georgiana's home, and the sisterly love that grew between her and Elizabeth was exactly what Darcy had hoped to see. Georgiana had the highest opinion in the world of Elizabeth, though at first she often listened with astonishment to her lively, joking way of talking to the brother for whom she, as a much younger sister, felt so much respect.

Lady Catherine was extremely angry at the marriage of her nephew, and expressed her feelings in a letter so insulting to Elizabeth that for a time all friendly connections were ended. The Collinses removed to Lucas Lodge until the storm had blown over, which it did at last, when Elizabeth persuaded her husband to offer to end the quarrel.

With the Gardiners they had always the warmest relationship. Darcy, as well as Elizabeth, really loved them, and they both felt most grateful towards the persons who, by bringing her to Derbyshire, had been the means of uniting them.

ACTIVITIES

Chapters 1–4

Before you read

1 Think about the title of the book. What are the possible causes and effects of:

a pride? b prejudice?

2 Find these words in your dictionary. They're all in the story.

carriage   lodge   parsonage   regiment

Match these groups of people with the four new words.

Which group might you find in each place?

_____ **a** soldiers, captain, commander

_____ **b** passengers, travellers, driver

_____ **c** husband, wife, children

_____ **d** priest, Christian minister, church secretary

3 Check the meaning of these words in your dictionary.

agreeable   engaged   inferior   lively   noble

Complete each sentence with one of the new adjectives.

a Mr. Gordon was an .... host. He was pleasant to everybody.

b The boys and girls were exhausted after the .... dance.

c His work is always .... to mine.

d The .... couple went to the jeweller's to look at rings.

e People throughout the country respected the king because he had a .... character.

4 Find these three verbs in your dictionary:

acquaint   astonish   neglect

Add *-ment*, *-ance* or *-ful* to the new words to complete the conversations. Look at your dictionary for help.

a A: I've lost my job.

   B: Why? What happened?

   A: My boss said I was .... of my duties.

b A: Mr. Brown, please meet an .... of mine.
   This is Miss Ward.

   B: Nice to meet you, Miss Ward.

c A: What happened?

   B: To my ...., a man jumped off that bridge.

After you read

5 Name:

  a Mr Bennet's daughters (in order of age).

  b Mr Bennet's heir.

  c Mr Bingley's proud friend.

  d Elizabeth's best friend.

  e the nearest town to Longbourn.

6 Who is the speaker? What are they talking about?

  a 'What a fine thing for our girls!'

  b '. . . I could easily forgive *his* pride, if he had not wounded mine.'

  c '. . . you must be two of the silliest girls in the country.'

  d 'They were brightened by the exercise.'

  5 'I am conscious, madam, of the injustice to your lovely daughters . . .'

7 Discuss how men and women of this period and class seemed to spend their time. What forms of social behaviour were important?

Chapters 5–10

Before you read

8 How successful do you think a marriage between Mr Collins and Elizabeth Bennet would be? Why?

9 Find these words in your dictionary:

  g*odfather* *heir* *relief* *scorn*

  a Which word means a person who might give advice?

  b Which word means a person who might expect to receive some money?

  c Describe three pairs of people who might *scorn* each other.

  d We may feel *relief* when a difficult situation ends. Think of one or two examples of situations like this.

After you read

10 How does:
- **a** Mr Wickham describe Mr Darcy?
- **b** Mr Bingley describe Mr Wickham?
- **c** Mrs Bennet view a possible marriage between Elizabeth and her cousin?
- **d** Mr Bennet view the same possibility?
- **e** Jane view Mr Bingley's departure from Netherfield?
- **f** Charlotte Lucas view her own marriage?
- **g** Mrs Gardiner feel about a possible marriage between her niece and Mr Wickham?
- **h** Elizabeth feel about Mr Wickham's relationship with Mary King?

11 Play the parts of Elizabeth and Mr Wickham at Mrs Philips's house. Discuss your feelings about Mr Darcy.

12 Play the parts of Elizabeth and Mr Collins on the occasion of Mr Collins's proposal of marriage.

Chapters 11–16

Before you read

13 What hope is there now for a relationship between:
- **a** Jane and Mr Bingley?
- **b** Elizabeth and Mr Wickham?

14 Check the meaning of these words in your dictionary:

colonel   prejudice

- **a** In what ways do you think *prejudices* can hurt people in a school or in a neighbourhood?
- **b** Do people in your country respect people with titles like *colonel*? Why not?

After you read

15 Who:
   a travels with Elizabeth to visit Mr and Mrs Collins?
   b 'looks weak and disagreeable'?
   c asks Elizabeth her age?
   d is invited to use the housekeeper's piano at Rosings?
   e has 'saved a friend from the inconvenience of a most unwise marriage'?
   f 'is all beauty and goodness'?
   g is in love in spite of his best attempts to be sensible?
   h did Mr Wickham almost persuade to run away with him?
16 Discuss the reasons why Mr Darcy would prefer not to be in love with Elizabeth. How much sympathy do you have with his anxieties?
17 Imagine that you are Elizabeth. Tell your sister Jane, at your next meeting, about Mr Darcy's proposal and the range of emotions you felt at that time.

Chapters 17–22

Before you read

18 Explain why Elizabeth now feels she has been 'blind, prejudiced, unreasonable'.

After you read

19 Why:
   a is Lydia so happy to receive an invitation to Brighton?
   b is Wickham glad to leave Meryton?
   c did Mr Bennet marry his wife?
   d is Elizabeth worried about visiting Pemberley?
   e is Elizabeth interested in listening to the housekeeper at Pemberley?
   f are the Gardiners so surprised when Mr Darcy is polite to them?
   g is 26 November fixed in Mr Bingley's memory?
   h is Miss Bingley so rude to Elizabeth?
   i is Elizabeth so upset by Jane's letters?

j do Lydia's father and uncle travel to London?

k is Mr Collins's advice strange for a religious man?

l is Mr Bennet so severe to Kitty?

20 Do you agree with Elizabeth that 'in a time of such a misfortune as this, one cannot see too little of one's neighbours'?

21 Imagine you are one of these characters. Give your views on the causes and effects of Lydia's behaviour.

   a Mrs Bennet

   b Mr Bennet

   c Mr Darcy

   d Mr Collins

   e Jane Bennet

   f Elizabeth Bennet

Chapters 23–28

Before you read

22 How do you think the story will end for each of the main characters?

After you read

23 Answer questions about this part of the book.

   a Who marries whom?

   b Whose fortune makes one of the weddings possible?

   c Who is unhappy about one or more of the marriages?

24 'For what do we live, if not to amuse our neighbours and laugh at them in our turn?' What does Mr Bennet's remark tell us about his own character and attitudes? Do you agree with him?

25 Discuss how much you admire:

   a Mr Bennet, as a father.

   b Mrs Bennet, as a mother.

   c Mr Darcy, as a brother.

   d Jane Bennet, as a sister.

   e Mr Collins, as a church minister.

Writing

26 What part do pride and prejudice play in the development of the story?

27 Write both the letter in which Lady Catherine expresses to Mr Darcy her feelings about his proposed marriage, and her nephew's response to it.

28 Compare the marriages of two of the Bennet sisters. How suited are the women to their partners? Which marriage is likely to be more successful?

29 Which character do you find the most unpleasant? Explain why.

30 Explain why you would or would not have enjoyed the kind of lifestyle led by the Bennets, Bingleys and Darcys.

31 What do you think are the reasons for the book's continuing popularity?

Answers for the Activities in this book are published in our free resource packs for teachers, the Penguin Readers Factsheets, or available on a separate sheet. Please write to your local Pearson Education office or to: Marketing Department, Penguin Longman Publishing, 5 Bentinck Street, London W1M 5RN.